Confessions *of a*
DIVISION-1 ATHLETE

A Dad and Daughter's
Guide to Survival

JIM KARAS and **OLIVIA KARAS**

Published by High Sign

Library of Congress Cataloging-in-publication data is on file with the publisher.

Cover Design: Adept Content Solutions

Photo Credits
Front Cover: Emily Howell-Forbes
Insert page 1: Michigan Athletics
Insert page 4, left: Michigan Athletics
            right: John Strong
Insert pages 5, 6, 7 (with the exception of the photo of Evan and Olivia): Michigan Athletics
Insert page 8: Tyler Meisinger

ISBN softcover: 978-1-63848-851-4
ISBN ebook: 978-1-63848-852-1

FIRST EDITION
Printed in the United States of America by Color House Graphics, Grand Rapids, Michigan

www.karasconfessions.com

CONTENTS

ACKNOWLEDGEMENTS
Jim Karas

First, I would like to thank Nancy Hancock, who has now officially edited three-and-a-half books for me. The half is a story so let's skip that and just say four. She has always brought clarity and shape to my books, but this one in particular just "fit" for both Olivia and for me. She got us. She got our humor. She got our goal and message. As a former dancer and theater director, Nancy also understands the physical and emotional toll of performing and putting yourself "out there," which is an underlying theme throughout our book. Nancy, "thank you." This won't be our last project together, so stay tuned.

Second to Baba. Olivia and I learned a lot about your experience as the sibling of an athlete. As your dad, it was hard to read. What was not hard was your ability to very clearly explain the situation, both as a child and then as a growing and evolving teenager. You are going to help a lot of families with your honesty. I've already discussed it with a number of parents who currently have a similar situation, such as one child in the spotlight and the other not so much. Just know, there is a "Dad and Son" project out there. I already have some ideas. I promise you, even when you are building and running an international, luxury, adventure hotel chain (Baba's dream), we will sit down and write as I want that same experience with you as I had with Olivia. I also expect a good deal on your best hotel suite!

Third, to the people who sat through countless, sometimes brutal (at least in the club years) gymnastic competitions. That was by definition, an "act of love." And for those who both bought and then wore the Michigan garb at meets – wow! Thank you for keeping me company and making Olivia feel so special.

Finally, to Olivia. Thank you for putting up with me and buckling down to get this project done. Thank you for allowing me to "speed skate." That's what I do when I'm stressed or getting punchy or antsy. I don't do it on the ice. I just stand up and start the motion of speed skating. I also do some ridiculous dance moves. Sometimes, Olivia joined me. Talk about sweet or equally nuts…

Pokey (her nickname), I didn't know you before this project. I mean, I knew you as my daughter, the athlete, the frequent goof ball, the student and the friend, but I really didn't understand what makes you tick and gives you confidence or, quite honestly, not so much confidence. As a writer, I thought you would be good, as I've read some of your previous schoolwork. I just didn't know you would be "this" good. What a gift. How special!

Evan and Olivia, I frequently refer to you both as my "air." I don't know how I would get through the approximate 40,000 breaths I take each day without you…

ACKNOWLEDGEMENTS
Olivia Karas

My journey writing this book wouldn't have been possible if it weren't for a few very special people.

Dad, thank you for believing in me as a writer and pursuing this project with me. I remember when this was all just an idea, and here we are. Not many people can work closely with their dad on a project out of pure joy and love of a shared passion. I feel this has given us the relationship we never got to have while we were both always working on our own passions. Now, we found our shared love and ran with it. Writing this book with you has been the best way to get to know you more and just hang out with you both as my dad and as my bestie who always reminds me to "persevere." Thank you for all of the writing dates, laughs, interpretive dances, Speedway iced tea stops, command position conversations and high signs. Can't wait for our final one in the future right before we take a special walk. We make one hell of *a team.*

Mom, I am lucky to have a woman with such strength, dignity and work ethic as my role model, mom and friend. I wake up every day thankful that you taught me to stand up for what I believe in and fight for the ones I love. And to use my passions and voice for good, like writing this book. Thank you for showing us at a young age how to make positive changes for your happiness, raise two children while working tirelessly and kicking ass at all of it. Plus, you make an unreal Thanksgiving dinner, so thanks for that, even though it has nothing to do with this book. I feel empowered to share my voice and demand change because of the example you set for me.

To my baby brother, Evan. Although we have had our bouts of biting each other and fighting, we always fought out of love. While writing this, I wondered what my life would be like without a little brother, who happens to also be one of my best friends, and I can't imagine the boredom I would feel. Your energy and devotion shines in everything you do and your passion for being your best self as a friend, an athlete, a son, a brother and a person is infectious. Thank you for being my rock, supporting me through it all and truly being the reason I bought into writing. And thank you for all of the loud cheers at meets. I can't wait to do the same for you while watching you dominate at Cornell.

Finally, to the sport of gymnastics. Though you have destroyed my limbs, gave me a new Achilles, took my ligaments in my right ankle, caused me severe back pain and gave me trap muscles that simply will not leave, without you, none of this would have happened. And despite the pain you may have left me with, thank you for allowing me to feel like I could fly, bringing me my best friends, and engraining life lessons and ultimate resume building traits in me. Most importantly, thank you for ending when I turned 22 and graduated so I could pursue this next chapter of my life.

INTRODUCTION

According to author Dr. Meg Meeker, a pediatrician with more than thirty years experience counseling girls:

> A young woman's relationship with her father is far more important than we've ever realized. An active father figure is maybe the single most important factor in a young woman's development. To become a strong, confident woman, a daughter needs her father's attention, protection, courage, and wisdom.

It's been a journey for us both. Many high highs, just as many low lows. Personally, professionally, you name it. Can't say we have learned it all, but at this point we collectively have eight-two years (I'm sixty; Olivia is twenty-four) under our belt. I'm not saying we are experts at any of this. Let's just say we have some history and experience.

We thought, *What if we had a roadmap before this all began?* And we mean a roadmap from:

Birth,
    To "Mommy and Me" class,
        To the gym and the training—daily, constantly, relentlessly,
        To the coaches,
            To club competitions
            To scholarships
            To Michigan,
                To the teams, ever evolving,
                To where we are today?

Would it help others?

Would it help us process this chapter in our lives?

We decided to write. Actually, we had to write. We have talked about doing a project together for a long time. There was never time for Olivia to do anything outside of school, training, and competing: lather, rinse, repeat. This is going to be our exercise, a different exercise than I have written about previously. I've had books published in the past about weight loss, fitness, energy levels, and anti-aging. I was one of the first personal fitness trainers in Chicago back in 1987 when most people didn't know what a personal trainer was. In the past thirty-three years, I then went on to build a team of trainers and open fitness and wellness studios. This is clearly a departure for me as it's not just a "how to" book, as mine have been in the past. Our goal with this book is to make sense of our journey together and maybe, just maybe, by sharing our experience we help people navigate not only the athlete piece, but also the whole parent/child, or in our case, dad/daughter relationship.

Fun fact: we both learned a *ton*. Olivia would read me a chapter (we found reading aloud to be hugely beneficial), and I'd say, "What? I never knew that," or I never really knew the whole extent of the situation. Same happened to her when I shared the *E True Hollywood* version of the past, which I either forgot to share or was actively trying to forget.

Look, as parents, we sometimes feel it is best to protect our child from all the facts. There is no reason a child needs to always know what is going on behind the scenes. The pressure on them is likely immense. The fun part about having a twenty-four-year-old daughter is communicating with an adult, not a hissing, impatient toddler, a hormonal, stressed-out teen, or overly pressured college student.

The other truth about this project? We never spent a lot of time together. Olivia was at school or the gym and I was working seven days a week. Both of our schedules were constantly busy. Since Olivia's graduation from University of Michigan in May 2019, we've been together, face to face, more than we ever have before. Wait, one exception.

Ellen, Olivia's mom, was a stage actress until Olivia was ten. Actually, an award-winning actress who worked all over the country. When we would travel to see her in a play, I have a rule—only the big seat. Sorry if this sounds obnoxious, but I've traveled over two million miles in the past thirty-plus years, and I feel I've earned the right. Lucky for me, Olivia was very small when she was little. You can have a child on your lap until they are two. Olivia was "two" until she was almost five. I would tell her, "If someone asks your age, tell them you are two," and she stated in her fiercely, independent voice, "But Daddy, I'm four and a half." I said, "Yes, but for the next two hours, play this game with me and be two."

We also learned in the past months some additional odd similarities. You will learn of Olivia's popped right Achilles during a competition. I partially tore mine, not from an accident but because of minamist gym shoes I was wearing for work and workouts. At a recent physical, we found out we both have slightly enlarged thyroid glands and almost identical total cholesterol and good-to-bad cholesterol ratios. Odd. How many fathers and daughters go to the same doctor on the same day for "daddy/daughter" physicals? Probably not many you know.

This also has been a special time that happened partly by planning and partly by circumstances. After a rough couple of years at my firm, the demands on my time were alleviated since I hired a new, competent COO to run my business and Olivia chose to hunker down in Chicago and actively look for a job rather than running around Europe, as many of her friends did. It definitely has been a bonding time, and I know I'm a better parent, friend, and coworker as Olivia has taught me to be a better listener. I actually shut up and take it in, as she has a unique perspective on people, relationships, and situations. I didn't know this in the past because I didn't get the one-on-one time, and I rarely shut up. I've had solo time traveling with her brother, Evan, but the demands of her sport, coupled with my heavy work load, shut down the opportunity. I'm grateful we found this time because hopefully soon, she will start her new career, or my career will once again pivot. The window to spend this precious time when we could look deeply together on all that has occurred since she went to her first "Mommy and Me" gymnastics class when she was five and put on her first leotard.

We came up with our title "Confessions of a Division-I Athlete," as many years ago, I was writing for the "SPLASH" section of the *Chicago Sun-Times*. I could cover whatever I was interested in at the time, and I wrote a question-and-answer article entitled "Confessions of a Rio Wannabe" with Olivia. At that time, the Olympics were on the table. We had a blast writing the piece, and it literally took all of ten minutes. The content was basically me asking her simple questions and her responding with simple, honest, often funny answers. Both Ellen and Olivia's coach, Olga (not her real name, and you will understand why later) were somewhat put off by the piece, as Olivia used some "colorful" language. But hey, it was honest, and that's what made it fun and relatable. Of course, the "interview" took place in our kitchen with me typing the answers in real time at our kitchen island while Olivia sat on the counter with her feet up and her arms wrapped around her knees, which is her happy place.

Soon thereafter, Olivia was asked to give a speech at a mother/daughter event hosted by my friend and client at the time. She was asked to share her experience as an athlete to the moms and young girls attending. About a week before, Olivia said to me, "Dad, I'm nervous; what am I supposed to say?" I said, "Give it some thought, I will give it some thought, and let's see what we come up with."

As a former *ABC News* contributor and host of my own cable TV show, I had an idea I wanted to run by our hostess, then Olivia. I said, "What if instead of a speech, I interview her?" Hostess loved it. Olivia loved it, but the rule was she would not know the questions in advance.

I was going to get real and not just ask about her sport and her relationship to the sport, but our relationship, dating, school, her vile, hormonal behavior during some of her teenage years (oh boy, they were not pretty), all of it—unplugged.

It went really well. The best part was the following week when many of the moms shared, "My daughter and I had the best conversation on the way home in the car because your talk seemed to give her the confidence to open up and share things I didn't know. Then I asked questions I never imagined, and she answered." Cool. Our hope is that this book acts as a "vehicle," and you will understand why we choose this word and why "vehicle" is in quotes later.

An athlete's career has a beginning, hopefully a very long, fulfilling middle, and then for some, either an abrupt end (an injury) or imposed end, such as Olivia's graduation from Michigan. Our goal is to help both the parent and the athlete understand this is a joint endeavor and should be a joint decision.

Our subtitle, *A Dad and Daughter's Guide to Survival*, pretty much says it all. There is a lot to consider, whether you are the parent or the athlete.

To you, the athlete, I would ask:

1. Do you live for this sport, or are you just doing it for fun or because your friends do it?
2. Have you tried other sports or activities that may also be of interest to you or utilize your same physical and mental talents?
3. Do you want to focus on a physical talent, or are you also interested in debate or art or student council?
4. Are you well aware of the sacrifices, as there will most likely be many?
5. Big important question: are your parents making you do this or guilting you into pursuing this sport? Is this direction their dream or yours?

To you, the parent, I have to ask:

1. Are you sure this is the right direction for your son or daughter?
2. Have you exposed your child to a lot of different activities and interests?
3. Is this the right time to go "all in?"
4. Is this the right strategy to hopefully get into a better college or university?
5. Is this about scholarship money?

Then talk about it. Dig in. Don't gloss over the details because there are a lot you are going to learn about in subsequent chapters. These should be conscious, discussed choices and answers, not ones you simply fall into, like we did. It's provocative and doesn't always end the way you, the athlete, had hoped or you, the parent or parents had hoped. That's what makes it a guide to "survival."

For the record, I was a fat, smoking, theater and glee club geek in high school before anyone knew what glee club was. Watched no sports. Played no sports. Hated sports, as I was always the last person picked for a team because no one showed me how to catch a ball or throw a ball—any ball. I sucked. I knew zero about sports of any kind, even less than zero about university scholarships. I had no idea what I was getting myself into because Olivia's talent and drive took us to places previously unknown to me. I was basically clueless.

So here's what started happening when some random person would come up to me as Olivia progressed and started winning competitions and eventually earned a spot on the University of Michigan women's gymnastics team.

Random Person—"Wow, Olivia is going to be a D-I athlete."

Me—"Yeah. Cool!"

What was not cool was this fact: I didn't know what a D-I athlete was. For the record, D-I is a Division one athlete. There is also Division two and three, but one was, well, one. That's a BFD! Hopefully they didn't realize I had no clue what they were talking about. They probably did. Me bad.

Different Random Person—"Go Blue!" with fist raised.

Me again—"Yeah. Cool!"

What was not cool was this fact: no one told me this is what University of Michigan alumni and fans say in support of everything Michigan. Maize and blue are their colors. That's where the "Go Blue!" comes from. "Go Blue!" is a universal phrase to show solidarity and excitement for everything Michigan. By uttering this phrase, you instantly make a connection with people who either went to Michigan or are huge fans. This also happens when you see the frequent Michigan attire, worn by some at all times, regardless of age or appropriateness. I thought they were commenting on my blue blazer or blue jeans, part of my standard uniform. Again, me bad.

I went to the University of Pennsylvania. It wouldn't cross my mind to go up to someone in a Penn t-shirt or hat and say, "I went there too." I have to say it is different with Michigan alumni. They just appear so insanely proud. I now go up to someone in Michigan attire and immediately say, "My daughter graduated from there," and the conversation is off and running. I like being a Michigan parent, or "Michigan Dad," as it says on my official t-shirt you will learn about later. I admire those who are so deeply attached to this institution.

As I previously wrote, we are now at the end of Olivia's career. As you are about to learn in chapter 1, she's done and ready for the next challenge. As you read on, we are going to take turns with the narrative, sometimes with a necessary interjection here and there. We will revisit old conversations and situations and also share some shocking new conversations and revelations. Also, we didn't write this in chronological order. We thought it was more fun and more relatable to jump between the past, the present, and the hopeful future and let our story unfold. Some of our "confessions" may also come as a surprise or may be unexpected. We want you to get to know us as people *and* as an athlete and the parent of an athlete.

What have we come up with? I don't know.

Maybe something to make you laugh,
 Maybe something to make you cry,
  Maybe something to give you direction and information,
   Or hopefully, something to get a
    conversation started you never expected.

Or maybe something to make you just stop and think. Think about what it means to be an athlete or the parent of one. Think about the sacrifices we will share that may not have crossed your mind. Think about how it may form and shape your relationship. Don't go into it blindly, as we did. Think.

We finally understand why we feel a specific way about certain people and situations, past and present. Don't gloss over important events. Talk about them.

We are Jim Karas and Olivia Karas, dad and daughter. We survived this important piece in both of our lives.

Now come listen in as we share our "confessions."

Chapter 1
I'M STRUCTURELESS

CONFESSION—*I'm going to be a cocktail waitress in a slutty red dress!*

That's what I said to Evan as I wept outside of a well-known Chicago restaurant on Oak Street in June 2019. A week prior, my dad and I were there, and the assistant manager said to us, "Do you happen to know of any women twenty-one or older looking for a part-time cocktail waitress job?" He finished his sentence looking directly at me. For some reason, it didn't bother me at the time but "bam," out of nowhere, I walked past the front door today and burst into tears. I kept repeating, "I'm going to be a cocktail waitress in a slutty red dress." I couldn't help but think, *Four years of college and sixteen years of gymnastics and what? I'm in a slutty red dress with my boobs pushed up. Boobs I've spent years trying to hide and strongly dislike. Now I need them? Pushed up? To serve!*

Yes, I overexaggerated the situation, but this was real emotion. You will learn I am a person fully in touch with my many emotions. Yet this was one I had never felt before—failure.

My entire life had been structured around my gymnastics career. School, my parents' work and social life, Evan's life, holidays—everything was orchestrated so I could do gymnastics. I had a purpose and a playbook. No decisions. No options. No need to think about what comes next.

Now, I was a little stuck. Okay, not a little. A lot.

Let me breakdown the facts:

April 19, 2019. NCAA Prelim Championships. Potentially my last gymnastics meet ever, depending on if we advanced to the finals the next day. Here were the final scores for that meet:

- UCLA won with a 197.675.
- Louisiana State University took second place with a 197.5125.
- University of Michigan took third place with a 197.25, and we didn't advance.

We competed our hearts out and missed out on advancing to the finals by more than one quarter of a point and less than one-third of a tenth of a point, 0.2625! Our all-around team score was 197.25 out of a possible 200. Only the top two teams go on to compete in the finals. Lots of score talk later.

Just know that I've lived most of my life for scores. Long before others were getting star ratings and "likes" on social media, I was a gymnast tethered to the leaderboard, anxious to see what group of appearing numbers would determine my future. On this particular day, my last day as a competitive gymnast, basically, a toe point kept us away from the finals.

But these Nationals were the best finish we had during my time at Michigan, and we honestly did all that we could with the team members we had left that particular day. Sometimes it just isn't meant to be, and I was really okay with that. I'm proud of us as we got that close and fought through some huge obstacles, which my dad and I will later explain, throughout my senior year. At the end of the day in my final year, we finished in the top five at the NCAA Championships (FYI, that NCAA stands for National Collegiate Athletic Association). We had a remarkable season with so much to be proud of.

April 25, 2019. Classes end. I am done with my communications major and writing minor.

May 5, 2019. Graduation. Five thousand of us in our cap and gown on the field of The Big House, my university's famous football stadium. I'm no longer a Michigan student.

May 31, 2019. I move out of my house, my home for the past three years, and say "goodbye" to my Ann Arbor family.

The sport which defined my entire life: gone.

My best friends and housemates: gone.

My school, my place: gone.

My identity: gone.

Just about everything except my injuries and boobs: gone.

What wasn't gone was the anxiety I felt every day as I believed I no longer had "purpose." There's a haunting word. Purpose. As a gymnast, training gave me purpose. As a Michigan student-athlete, representing my school gave me purpose. Winning for Michigan, my coaches, and my team gave me purpose. Now, I feel I'm a washed-up former athlete searching for my new purpose. I just can't find it. Nothing "sticks."

I'm not stupid—I knew my gymnastics career would end at some point and I would need to explore my next calling. Think of it this way though: how many people do you know by the age of twenty-two who have already had a career and retired from it? It's a shocking fact, but for me, it's true.

My dad always jokes (or doesn't joke; sometimes I really cannot tell) that he is trying to figure out what he wants to be when he grows up. Mind you, he is sixty and has had a successful career as a #1 *New York Times* bestselling author, entrepreneur, speaker, and father. That is a career. We have a private family joke. Don't just call him *New York Times* bestseller because it drives him bananas. You have to say, "Number one." He goes on to say, "Do you call Meryl Streep an Academy Award nominee? No, you call her Academy Award winner because she won." In my opinion, my dad has had a big career. He doesn't feel that way. He, too, is looking for his "purpose." At least I'm not alone.

We all hear about the classic midlife crisis. Most of the time, you act on it: buy a sports car, decide to get in shape, quit your job, get a boob job, leave your spouse or partner, whatever. I need you to understand, my midlife crisis was happening at twenty-two. The difference is I had no choice but to pivot. Unlike many sports, gymnastics does not continue.

I laugh when I explain this fact to people and they say, "Can't you just continue part time and join a recreational league?"

Um, no. I'm beat up, still in pain, and want to live. Getting up on a beam and attempting a routine, without daily practice, could result in death. I'll pass.

That's why it doesn't continue.

Gymnastics is much different than other sports. We choose the Olympic or collegiate path, which I will discuss more later, and then follow it to the end. Similar to competitive ice skaters and dancers, our bodies get abused. But a skater can scale back his or her jumps and still enjoy the ice. A dancer may no longer perform "on point," or execute dramatic leaps and turns, but he or she can still dance. As a gymnast, once you are done, you are done. Plus, our bodies can't take much more pounding. You can't perform gymnastics "light." You either do it full out or not at all. And getting up on any of the four apparatus could be very dangerous once you are not spending six days a week training. Rarely do women exceed age twenty-two as a gymnast, and after college gymnastics, everyone is pretty much done. Except for Oksana Chusovitna, who is forty-four, has three children and is about to embark on her eighth Olympic games. I mean, how amazing for her as it is remarkable, but it's a "Hard No" for me. Evan started using this popular expression, and our family has adopted it. A "Hard No" means "Absolutely not" and "Don't ask me again!"

Other sports have different timelines. My good friend Robbie Mertz played soccer at Michigan and decided to leave school early to go pro. He finished his business degree and now plays in the Major League Soccer (MLS) league for the Pittsburg Riverhounds. He has been extremely successful. He had the option to continue the sport he grew up identifying with.

I guess I could try to go to the 2021 Olympics now, but I'm going to leave that to Oksana.

For any gymnast or parent of a gymnast reading, this sport will end abruptly. For many of my teammates and fellow competitors, it ended earlier than mine due to an injury or global pandemic—who would have thought? You will have mastered a skill and retired from it by the time you are twenty-two (if you are lucky) and will need to move onto the next stage of life. Be prepared—it comes quicker than you'd expect. Part of what makes it so abrupt is there is no time during holiday breaks or over the summer to begin your post-gymnastics playbook. We live, breathe, and sometimes almost die for gymnastics. Then, bye-bye. You're done.

I remember waking up the next morning after our last meet and immediately feeling like I was late for a team meeting or practice. I bet you assumed I would say I felt a sigh of relief, but I really didn't. My brain was programmed. Ever since I was six years old, there was always a practice to go to or a workout to complete. So, this day felt exactly like any other day. Except, I got to eat an In-N-Out burger and fries, guilt-free, as I did realize I didn't have to fit into an extra small leotard the next weekend. That was the biggest immediate shift in my reality.

FYI, it still hasn't settled in, and now it's almost nine months since my last competition. Odd, I know, as I just recently went back to Ann Arbor for my first Michigan meet and throughout the competition kept thinking, *We really need to get into the gym Monday to fix some of these errors. Why are we not sticking more landings?* I thought *we* as if I was still a part of the team. Maybe I need some therapy . . .

Why Is Gymnastics Unique?

Gymnasts don't get time off. Nor should we take any time off. Let's face it—this sport is a 24/7/365 sport with leeway only for a few major holidays. It is dangerous to inconsistently practice. It's got to stay in your DNA. Of course, success as an athlete in any sport increases with consistent training. But with gymnastics (and from what I've learned, ice skating), five days off could set you back as far as a whole month. Trust me . . .

Another reason to not take time off is our bodies are deteriorating with age and abuse. Many gymnasts may have not one, but two peaks in their career, myself included. I know that my "pre-puberty" peak was when I was twelve. At that point, I had five years of competing under my belt and was growing into my pre-puberty body as an athlete. Not to mention, pre-puberty meant no boobs, bloating, body image issues, or burning desire to burn calories. Just a general comfort in my adolescent skin and my athletic identity. Then my "post-puberty" peak happened during my last season, specifically the last few meets, which you will soon read about. Right at the end, I finally found my new sense of comfort, but this time in my matured skin and far more experienced athletic ability. I guess I consider myself lucky, as many gymnasts lose interest during their final season, either because they have simply peaked and are no longer competing at the same level with the same passion, or they are already thinking about the next chapter in their lives and are done.

But I have to add, at this point there was not a joint or muscle in my body that hadn't been compromised by injury or overuse. That's just what comes while nearing your career expiration date, which also makes consistent practice during your final years much more important. Here is an unwritten rule: gymnasts must devote their summers to training, recovering, and lifting on their respective college campuses. Sure, this is "voluntary," but I say it in quotes because, really, nothing in this sport is voluntary. I would say everything is "strongly suggested." According to the NCAA rules, a coach cannot require supervised workouts during the off-season. This gets tricky with gymnastics, as safety is a huge component. It really doesn't work to hand a gymnast the keys to a world-class gym for practice with no supervision. Ninety-five percent of the time we don't need much, but that 5 percent creeps up at the worst possible times, and it can be detrimental to you, the team, and the school. Because of this, coaches are allowed in the gym to watch summer practices. And let's face it, they keep track of what you do in the gym, how you look over the summer, and if you're religiously doing your specific, prescribed rehab exercises for who knows how many injuries.

Many collegiate athletes struggle with time for career planning during their junior and senior year, but it depends on the sport. I have friends who played field hockey, soccer, lacrosse, football, and so on and have a set season. In their off season, they are focusing on conditioning and staying in shape. They could have summer internships and jobs in other cities, then go to any gym to lift weights or run to stay in shape. It did not require supervision and, for most, not much equipment. Most of my fellow athletes had their preseason and season in the fall, beginning in August and ending in December. Then, they are done. After the holiday break, it was "find a job" time. They also had an athletics-free second semester with more party time, more networking time, more adjustment time, as school was ending, and, well, just more time.

What's a Job?

As I am writing this, I have moved to New York. I longed to move East. Actually, I needed a bigger launchpad, and I believed New York would give me that. I grew up in Chicago and went to school in Ann Arbor. I'm a Midwest girl in need of a "New York State of Mind." Both *Friends* and *Sex and the City* are my peeps. If Chandler Bing and Carrie Bradshaw had a one-night stand, I would be their love child. I say this because I have his goofy/witty sense of humor and her tenacity, drive, and—hopefully—her ability to write. They needed New York, and so do I.

My dad helped me rent a place in the East Village. I started my apartment search online. Apartments.com was my BFF. I had no clue what I was doing but wanted to prove to him I could put the work in. I would text him a link to a pad I desperately thought was "the one," and he would say, "Honey, it could be next to a crack den. You have to understand the neighborhood and then actually go see this place." After days of apartment searching on foot, extra-large iced Dunkin coffee in hand (no Starbucks for me), and the help of a good broker, I found "the one." I love it. It's a one bedroom so my dad can come in town and torture me, as he still has frequent business here. It's also close to Evan, as he's a freshman at the School of Hotel Administration at Cornell University (I know, a mouthful). That's in Ithaca, just a four-hour bus or train ride away. He and I are super close but haven't been close geographically because I was in Michigan, and he was at boarding school in Connecticut for the past four years.

This move also felt like a clean start. I had to rip the Band-Aid off. The Band-Aid was my ability to jump in my car and four hours later be back to my former life in Ann Arbor. I was doing this over the summer, and it just had to stop. My impromptu trips were stealing focus from all that was to come next. Ann Arbor was in my past. Moving to New York would take me into my future and remove the temptation to so easily revisit my past.

Funny, after all those years as a gymnast, I assumed my next step in life would just, you know, come *vaulting* toward me. I thought applying for a job and getting a job would be easy because I was told, "Everyone wants to hire D-I athletes," since prospective employers believe we have demonstrated the ability to successfully manage both school and our sport. D-I athletes are mostly considered achievers.

I was wrong.

JIM INTERJECTION: I live for all the "Squawk" programming about the stock market on CNBC. As I'm doing these final edits, the CEO of IBM, Ginni Rometty, has stepped down, and the commentators literally said, "The number of female CEOs has really taken a hit this last year. Ginni is the most recent loss. I hope companies start looking at former female athletes as they would be very successful in the top spot and we need more female leaders." I'm not kidding.

Confessions of a **DIVISION-I ATHLETE**

I did a little more digging and read that, according to research by Ernst & Young, 52 percent of all female C-suite level positions were athletes who played sports at the collegiate level. Once again, I was clueless as my life has been devoted to all things "business," but I never knew this correlation between athletics and business prevailed.

I have done all the classic stuff everyone is told to do when pursuing a job—network with as many people as possible, try to connect with someone even if you hardly know them but know of them, apply online, and move to New York for opportunities. And nothing.

The summer of 2019, I came home to Chicago for a forty-eight-hour training session for a part-time job. I was working for a terrific friend and client of my dad's, Seth Deutsch. Seth and I have many similarities in our journeys, as he, too, was a D-I athlete. Also, a frequently injured athlete. Translation—He gets me. We all had dinner in the early summer. He told me he would help me figure out my next "purpose." After a couple months of misery, he offered me a part-time sales position. I took it without hesitation. I cold called and emailed business owners in the heating, ventilation, and air conditioning (HVAC) space, as Seth's company wants to acquire them.

After the training, I went home to my dad's apartment in the city and sat in the "command positions." These are two comfortable, matching armchairs in his bedroom. Dad's armchair is in the corner, clearly the "throne," which he sits in all the time. I would never consider sitting in it. His swivels so he can see the TV, the view of the lake, and the person in command position two. I always sat in seat two, which, FYI, does not swivel. For some reason, my dad was cheap and decided his only needed to swivel and didn't spend the extra few hundred dollars to enable seat two to do so. Many important Karas conversations have taken place in these positions, frequently with white wine, "spicy" water—which is what I called his sparkling water when I was little—and popcorn. Always popcorn, a Karas staple made the old-fashioned way in a pot on the stove.

Come to think of it, the "command positions" are to the Karas family as "Central Perk" and the unnamed coffee shop were to *Friends* and *Sex and the City*.

Glass of Joel Gott Sauvignon Blanc in hand, things should have been good, at least good enough. I was home. I felt safe. I was sitting with my dad. At that time, I actually did have a bit of a purpose with my part-time job, another part-time job at an elite gym close to my New York apartment, and the work on this book. Instead, I cried. Burst into projectile tears from feeling so weak and helpless. I looked at my life in a very "glass half empty" way. Once again, I felt like a failure, an emotion uncommon to me, big time!

Was It a Job?

I actually got my first "job" as a D-I athlete at the University of Michigan. It was a job, but "was it a job?" I was pushed to achieve perfection, excellence, and "wins" as their athlete, or may I say, their employee, as I was paid in tuition and room and board. My dad insists I tell you the tuition is tax-free, but he paid income tax on room and board. His father was an accountant. Talking "tax" was their jam. The fact you do have to pay income tax solidifies my point. It was a "job."

But, in an interview when asked, "What experience do you have in this field?" I look at them like a deer in headlights, as I am sure many new graduates do. But I had no experience interviewing. I never had a summer internship. Never had time to explore, travel, or experience much outside of the gym and school.

I would think to myself:

I can do a beam routine with a leotard riding up my ass and act like nothing is wrong—does that count as experience?

I can think fast. You have to when you tweak your right shoulder during warm-up on bars and have to figure out how to compensate on your giants (that's when you go all the way around the top bar) using predominately your left shoulder. Stay balanced? Sure. Act like nothing is wrong? I can do that.

I can whip a floor routine together after a torn Achilles, when I'm not supposed to compete in floor for another couple of weeks. What do you do when your coach, who is your boss, looks at you after a fellow teammate/coworker is in pain and it isn't safe for her to continue to compete? My four-year Michigan gymnastics coach, Bev Plocki, put her arm around me as we walked to this next event and said, "Can you throw a floor routine together and get out there?"

At the time, I had been cleared to do gymnastics now for eleven months and was physically ready for any routine, even floor. My Achilles and foot had successfully healed. My coaches and athletic trainer, Lisa Hass, made sure I took my time physically coming back. I was ready, but I hadn't done the tumbling pass I tore my Achilles on in practice yet. Despite that, I had done everything else on the floor, even a watered-down (easier) last pass. The problem was, I was mentally freaked out as I hadn't done a floor routine in competition yet. But, being confident and brave was my job.

"Sure I can." That's my job.

The best advice I ever received was from a Michigan alum who used to work with my dad's very good friend, Jana Delancey, at MasterCard. She told me to translate my athletic experience into desirable employment traits both on my resume and in interviews. It took a while for me to relive my gymnastics years, specifically in college, and translate what I learned as an athlete to qualities many employers look for. Here is what I came up with:

1. Teamwork—I barely had any teammates during my club years, as most of the girls at my gym quit in high school or barely trained. But at Michigan, I accomplished working as a team with twelve to sixteen hormonal women for four years. And each year had a totally different

vibe and team dynamic as seniors graduated and freshmen joined. With new personalities came new team drama, and injuries always prevailed and dictated who was competing that day in which events.

2. Structure—I can get up at 6:30. Lift at 7:00. Start my first class at 8:30. Practice at 2:00, then dinner at 6:00. Most nights studying, or in season, packing because we might be leaving right after school for a meet on the weekend.

3. Message—We were expected to "message," as athletes and ambassadors. We are a brand. The brand is Michigan. We had a very specific platform through social media with a mission to drive attendance and attention to an upcoming meet, to the sport, and to the school. We were also expected to do it personally. Walking into a room full of strangers representing my school didn't scare me, as I did it often. Approach a person or group, introduce myself and strike up conversation. I had to sign autographs, take pictures with fans and alumni, and then more and more chit chat. Sometimes I was part of the recruiting process for prospective team members. That's why the cold calling and emailing for Seth doesn't scare me. Find the connection with someone, either in person, on the phone, or in an email and take it from there. I learned that skill and can do it with sincerity and a smile.

4. Loyalty—I was 100 percent loyal to the Michigan Athletic Department, and specifically, the women's gymnastics team.

5. Confidentiality—As you will learn, our team had some not so pleasant issues during my four years. I know how to keep our business, our business.

I have experience. I just hadn't quite learned how to translate it into a job description.

I also have tremendous grit, which I have no idea how to communicate to others. I've torn my Achilles, then had surgery. Before that, wrist surgery, a tonsillectomy, a broken back, and a broken heart by a few relationships. I've had weight and body image issues, which I will delve into later. And I've excelled in one of the most competitive sports that fulfilled my passions, gave me my best friends, and let me study what excited and interested me.

But now, I was lost and confused about what would come next. What would drive me the way gymnastics did? What career would give me the same butterflies and adrenaline "high" I felt when I competed? How was I going to meet and make all new friends in the working world after having built industrial-strength relationships with my teammates and other D-I athletes, as we shared the same sport and/or passion? No one tells you how to maneuver life after gymnastics or any sport that defined you and structured your life. You just do it.

Chapter 2
IT'S HAPPENING

CONFESSION—*I was clueless . . .*

It was the summer between Olivia's sophomore and junior year at the Latin School of Chicago. She had just turned sixteen in April. I got a phone call from Ellen. She said Scott Sherman, the associate coach of the University of Michigan women's gymnastics team, wanted Olivia to call him when she got home.

Recruiting sidebar: NCAA rules forbid a college or university coach to directly reach out to an athlete. The athlete had to initiate the interaction. Now, to be transparent my fellow parents and athletes, Michigan started sending physical letters to Olivia when she was in eighth grade after an all-around fifth-place finish at 2011 nationals, held in Long Beach, California. Under the regulations, paper interaction was allowed, but phone communication was not. A fifth-place finish was good, but I didn't know it would put her on the radar since I didn't know what "on the radar" even meant. Ellen and I had no idea they were courting her because she was only fourteen at the time. We just thought it was nice. Parents, take note. If a university writes to your athlete early on, they have already "swept right" on your son or daughter. They are watching and tracking. They may already have your child's name on some grid of potential recruits for specific positions in the coming years. These rules are updating constantly, so now with heightened social media interaction, the rules continue to evolve. Find out what is currently considered okay and not okay. Don't get in trouble or miss an opportunity.

Olivia interjection: I was the national first alternate. I did not make the national team because at the big regional competition three weeks prior, I fell in my fu&%ing beam routine. You are going to learn a lot about my "beam blues" later. My mom got a call that one of the girls who made the team broke her leg in practice. I was next in line. Nationals, here I come!

We had no idea the process would start this early. Olivia was just finishing eighth grade. How could we have imagined that the single-page congratulatory letter we received in the mail from the University of Michigan was actually their first "we are interested" communication? We were clueless because no one else at Olivia's gym had gone through the college recruiting process before. Huneth Lor, a former Michigan gymnast, was briefly working as an administrator at Olivia's gym. She gave us a lot of guidance. At the time, Olivia was the oldest gymnast at her gym because many of her fellow gymnasts dropped out once high school, boys, a social life, and so on prevailed over the rigors of training and competing. Her coach, who successfully competed for the Soviet Union, knew nothing about collegiate gymnastics and scholarships. No roadmap or path to follow. We were the guinea pigs.

While the interest was there, I made it clear to her: your education comes first, your sport second. Stanford was interested in her but informed us Olivia had to have a minimum 34 ACT (out of a perfect 36, not my girl) and predominately be taking AP courses (also not my girl).

What this did look like was a young, talented, uber-smart gymnast with *no* life, *no* balance, and probably a tiger mom lurking over her—nonstop. Of course, there could be exceptions, but it would be a terrible fit for Olivia because she would be on a team with this type of athlete, student, and parent. Mind you, she is smart, but not that 34 on her ACT kind of smart. AP courses, plus twenty-three hours each week at a gym? Nope, not the right place for her.

I recall a conversation early on when it came to this issue of scholarships, schools, and teams. I flat-out said, "You don't need to go where the scholarship money is. You can 'walk on' (which means join the school's team, if approved, without any financial incentive from the institution), and I will take care of the cost."

"No," she shot right back, definitely a "Hard No." "I want them to want me as much as I want them." This was said with wide eyes and a finger pointing right at me, only the second time I ever saw this side of Olivia. I was impressed with her conviction and her clear mindset. She knew what she wanted—"I want them to want me as much as I want them." I thought, *Go Olivia!*

Olivia interjection: Michigan felt like the right fit for me. They had a great team and coaches; I was closely following them my freshman and sophomore years, and they had a far more realistic view of academic requirements. They required a 25 on the ACT. Realistic. Didn't get it on my first attempt. Then, after a decent amount of tutoring (I am *not* a good standardized test taker and twice, VISA called my dad as they assumed the tutoring charges from my test center may have been fraudulent), I got it. Plus, Ann Arbor was close to home, but not *too* close to home. It had the academics, the athletics, the fandom, the passion, the beauty, the tradition, and Zingerman's deli. I mean, it sounded ideal.

Back to my story. It was a Friday night, and Olivia didn't drive home from the gym until about 9:00 p.m. Since she was six, six days a week, with maybe one week a year off, Olivia was at the gym. Monday through Friday practice was from 4:30–8:30 p.m. and Saturdays from noon—3:00 p.m. Do the math. Again, that's twenty-three hours a week, every week and was sometimes longer. That didn't include traffic and the time it took to physically get her there and back. Looking more like a career now, right?

Sitting in my command position, I watched outside my bedroom window as she pulled into the driveway of our building, and I met her right as she got off the elevator.

"Olivia, you need to make a phone call."

"Dad, can it wait? I feel gross. I just had the hardest conditioning session at practice and need to take a shower."

"Your call is to Scott Sherman from Michigan. Let's get this done. Do you want to go in my room and have privacy?"

"No, I want you and Baba (our nickname for Evan) in there with me."

We sit in the aforementioned command and first officer positions. Again, no swivel for her. Olivia put the call on speakerphone, which Scott didn't know. I had no idea what to expect:

"Olivia, how was practice?"

"Oh, I had a good day and am feeling strong,"

"How is your back?" Olivia, like many student athletes, has suffered way too many injuries, which we will share later. The big one at the time was a fractured back.

Confessions of a **DIVISION-I ATHLETE**

"Oh, it's much better, and I'm almost 100 percent."

Then a little more banter for about a minute about training and school.

Here comes the money question:

"Olivia, how would you like to be a Wolverine?" which is the mascot for the University of Michigan's athletic teams. FYI, I had no idea what he was saying. I thought Hugh Jackman, my friend and former client, was "Wolverine." Why would he ask Olivia to be one? I didn't think there could be two . . .

No pause: "Scott, that's my dream."

"Does that mean you accept?"

"Yes."

That's how it started.

What a moment. When I'm having a "challenging" day and/or feeling low, I go right back to this place. I close my eyes, and I'm back sitting in my chair, reliving how Olivia's face lit up and her eyes welled up when Scott said, "How would you like to be a Wolverine?" It was such a moment, a clear "win." All those years of practice and competition, injuries, doctor's appointments, follow-up doctor's appointments, driving to the middle of nowhere for a meet and sitting there for hours and hours, missing parties, events, trips, the huge sacrifices Olivia made—all suddenly made sense. Frequently and unfortunately, I have glossed over these moments in my life, but not this one. I was fully present. It was the beginning of Olivia's next chapter. It was exactly what she wanted.

How rare and special is that?

Now, at the ripe age of sixteen and about to start her junior year in high school, she was banged up, the back fracture, probably *no* tendons in her right foot because she rolled it so many times, shoulder issues, wrist issues—a lot. One of my clients in his late seventies once observed, "At this point in life, it's patch, patch, patch." The same applies for many competitive athletes, regardless of age. You learn to live with a certain level of pain and injury, and you are always patching.

As the conversation with Scott continued a little longer, Baba started wildly jumping for joy on my bed, and I just sat in tears, which will be an ongoing theme. I'm a Pisces and have frequent crying jags. Olivia's gymnastics career has produced a lot of tears over the years, both for joy and the opposite of joy, for both of us. We proudly own them and don't apologize for the show of emotion. It's part of being a "Karas."

The decision was made. Olivia was going to the University of Michigan to join the women's gymnastics team. Full scholarship. I had no idea what that really meant outside of the fact that I didn't have to write a check for her college education.

Note to parents: Each sport is different. I get a few dozen calls a year from a parent of a gymnast regarding scholarships. Some of these girls are just beginning eighth grade but are already being offered full rides. It is different for every sport, according to NCAA rules. Use caution since by the time your son or daughter is ready to decide on his or her college or university, he/she may have already quit or completely lost interest in their sport. But, because of the financial incentive, he/she feels obligated to once again embrace the sport for the money or the opportunity or the education. It's tough, especially for a young, not yet fully formed brain. It's equally tough for a parent who wants the best for their child, as this formerly loved sport may be the ticket. This "Golden Ticket," a reference from *Willy Wonka*, represents an opportunity, possibly a huge opportunity, even though the love and passion may be long gone.

Second note to parents: Certain sports, such as football and men's basketball, demand a lot of the scholarship money allocated to men. As per Title IX NCAA rules (they have a lot of them), women do receive the same

Confessions of a **DIVISION-I ATHLETE**

amount of scholarship money as men. Meaning, the big-player heavy sports like football and basketball eat up a lot of the scholarship money for the guys. For the girls, there are sports with less athletes on the roster, making for a more even divide of the allocated scholarship money. Yes, the football and basketball players get the majority of the boy's money, since alumni donations are often influenced by a winning team. It's a business decision for the school. So, parents and male athletes, remember my questions in the introduction. If your goal is a full or partial scholarship, be aware of which sports are receiving the most scholarship dollars. Do some research because this information may change. For example, as of 2018, the number of female high school rowers was 4,242, and there were at that time 2,080 scholarships. Remember, in operation "Varsity Blues," which is the ongoing college admissions scandal involving numerous celebrities and powerful parents, two very well-known "participants" were recruited for the USC crew team yet had never actively participated in the sport. Olivia shared with me that at Michigan, the men's soccer team only had approximately 9.9 scholarships one year and twenty-eight guys to divide it between. You do the math.

As Olivia hung up the phone, no injury, setback or sacrifice was on her mind. She was going to be on the woman's gymnastics team at the University of Michigan—and yes, now she joined me in tears, on and off, throughout the night, every time a family member or friend immediately came over that night to celebrate the news and congratulate her.

She "did it."

Chapter 3
THE EARLY SIGNS

CONFESSION—*It was Olivia's way or the highway.*

Let me take you back to much earlier years and some pretty blaring early signs.

Timeliness

Olivia had an annoying habit as a child and teenager. She was always early and expected you to operate on her clock. I vividly remember her pattern every morning before school. We would leave at 7:35 a.m. for Olivia's and Baba's first class at 8:00 a.m. at Chicago City Day, which they both went to through eighth grade. She would sit in the foyer, backpack on (and she would wear it on her back in the car, with a seatbelt on, sitting pitched forward, also annoying) at 7:25, making both irritating faces, which included nostrils flaring, and exasperating noises. I was, like, "Olivia, we leave at 7:35; you know that. Why are you rushing us?" No change. 7:25 backpack on. Stubborn.

Her brother was a hot mess. Typical boy. Comes out of his room with one shoe, one sock, the same filthy Sponge Bob t-shirt he wore the day before, now taken out of the laundry. No toothbrush had entered his mouth, and his hair looked like a rooster's because it always stuck straight up. It was an ongoing challenge, and while I'm trying to get him out the door, she's snarling and muttering under her breath, just loud enough so

I can hear her say, "We are going to be late." She was even worse when it came to getting to the gym on time after school. This way pre-WAZE. There was no way of knowing what traffic was going to be like as she was constantly being shuttled back and forth from a gym.

I should have known this was a sign of her impending behavior and character—impatient, always early, and stubborn. It was Olivia's way or the highway.

Okay, I will "out" myself. Me too. I share a penchant for being impatient, early, and somewhat stubborn. DNA or did she learn it from my behavior? I guess we will never know.

Fact—she was born early, two and a half weeks early. Ellen and I lived in downtown Chicago on Michigan Avenue. A client and friend had suddenly passed away and the visitation, the Shiva (he was Jewish), was just three blocks away.

Ellen, pregnant with Olivia in her thirty-seventh week, was walking slowly and uncomfortably. Anyone who knows me knows I don't understand anything slow, nor does Olivia. You should get out of the way if you ever see a black Honda CRV with Olivia behind the wheel. It's like the movie *Speed*, complete with screaming, honking, faces, and gestures. As we were walking, I could see Ellen was just done with the bloating, the weight, the pressure, the constant peeing, ugh. I've heard this over and over again from women in the last weeks of pregnancy. There clearly was a storm a brewing. You could see it in the sky and feel it in the air. We stayed for a brief period of time to pay our respects and then walked back home, once again, slowly, with a sense the coming storm was gaining momentum.

At 5:21 a.m. the next morning, Ellen nudges me and says, "Don't be startled. The phone is going to ring. My water broke, and I paged Lauren," our OB-GYN. Note pager kids. A pager, worn on your belt or in a pocket, was the way you got in contact with someone fast prior to everyone having cell phones. Very few people had cell phones in the early days of cellular revolution, and those were the size and weight of a brick. Ellen seems calm, but I could see in her eyes a sense of panic as I sit up and say, "Oh my God," still half asleep and in shock. "What do we do?"

"Take a shower. This won't move fast because it's my first." I quickly pop in the shower and think, *What is it going to feel like to hold my baby girl?* I still remember this moment.

We jump in a cab and whisk away to Prentice Woman's Hospital, just a mile away, a part of Northwestern Medicine and its crickets. Not a soul in sight. We get ushered into our promised private room, and even though Ellen's water had broken, nothing much is happening. We lie there, watch some mindless morning TV, and look at the storm continuing to grow outside. It is pitch black out, and FYI, I love a good storm.

A few hours later, I open the door to the hallway, and it is a madhouse. Think of an episode of *Grey's Anatomy* or another hospital drama when there has been a thirty-six-car pileup or a massive train wreck, and the place is out of control. Our assigned birthing nurse tells us that when a storm is approaching, the barometric pressure changes, and pregnant women pop—like crazy. This clearly was the case. Most women were not getting the lovely "promised" private room and instead were doubled up or even placed in overflowing surgical rooms.

Thank God Olivia was early. Either she had the wherewithal to kick the amniotic sac hard enough to break it, or she was doing some basic gymnastics moves to start the process early enough for us to get a good room. She probably instinctively knew. I'm a stickler when it comes to my choice of table at a restaurant. Maybe Olivia heard me, in utero, blowing a wingding when I didn't get what I wanted or was promised. It's feasible. Babies while in the womb do hear us. It's also possible she just had enough of the "inside" world and was more than ready to come out and join the action.

Finally, with the help of some Pitocin in the IV (which ordinarily the brain produces to start the delivery process, but sometimes you need a little extra hit to move things along) and an epidural, "it's happening." Ellen blows her nose and Olivia's head crowns and I say to Lauren,

"THERE IS A BABY IN THERE!"

"Yes," Lauren says calmly, "That's why we are here."

Finally, Olivia pops her head out, looks right at me as I'm ringside (can't imagine being anywhere else), lets out a powerful cry, and is ready to rock . . . and move.

I did get to hold her—amazing—the feeling. I realize, "I'm a dad."

Emotional

Post birth our first hard evidence of her temperament and need for soothing occurred around three months. Olivia was a colicky baby. For those of you who don't know what that means, think a lot of crying for no apparent reason. Three things would calm her down.

- I would hold her like a football, and play "flying baby," which included blasting music in the family room, frequently the overture of *West Side Story*—which if you don't know it, has tons of energy and movement—and wildly running around. She clearly liked the speed, the movement, and the loud music.

- Going to the building's indoor pool and holding her like a hovercraft just over the water and making the motorboat sound. She especially liked it when it was getting dark out, as she seemed mesmerized by the refection of the sun going down over the water, and then the lights. I had to keep moving, fast, or she would get irritated. I loved both of these activities because it was our first bonding time together.

- White noise. Olivia calmed down when the vacuum or blow dryer was on. When we turned one of them on, she was happy. Turned it off, screaming. Ellen was out of town, staying at a friend's house with Olivia, and she was uncontrollably crying through the night, keeping everyone up. Out of desperation, Ellen took Olivia into the bathroom (which was down the hall from the bedrooms) to turn on their blow dryer and placed it next to the sink as she held Olivia. It was on high for so long that the blow dryer literally sparked and lit on fire; then after Ellen threw it in the sink and doused the fire with water, it died. They were never asked back.

As I recall, we blew out our expensive vacuum cleaner from the excessive use and blew out more blow dryers than I can remember. To this day, Olivia works best with noise on in the background. All Karases do. We all have music on in either my home, Olivia's apartment, or Evan's dorm room, 24/7. Even to hotel rooms we bring our Bluetooth Bose speaker. None of us likes silence. Must be genetics or undiagnosed ADD.

Grit

Our second hard evidence foreshadowing her temperament and now her drive, occurred around seven months. Ellen was performing at the Arena Stage in Washington D.C. Someone had given us what we called "The Vehicle." That is why I put it in quotes in the introduction, as it plays an important role in establishing Olivia's drive and grit. "The Vehicle" was a Fischer Price triangular push toy on rollers. She would hold onto the back, like she was pushing a shopping cart, get on her tiptoes, and wildly race around our somewhat sad rental apartment in D.C. There was no walking. It was tiptoe running. When she would hit a corner, she would grit her teeth, turn, and look at us and hiss until we taught her how to pull back, turn it around, and continue terrorizing the carpeting. She never really sat around watching television or videos (Barney and only when she was sick) and pretty much was in perpetual motion.

Independence

Potty training was interesting. Given my profession, we didn't have junk food to eat in the house except for holidays or special occasions. No, we were not extreme. Both Ellen and I were simply aware of how diet effects concentration, mood, energy, behavior, and so on. When Olivia turned two, Ellen made the executive decision to potty train her in our Chicago apartment with a new technique she read about. She took Olivia's diaper off and placed numerous "potties" around the apartment. She rewarded Olivia with one jellybean for number one and two jellybeans for number two. She was trained in a day. Good! But there was a "not so good" result in that she insisted on flushing the toilet herself, every time. She would jump off the potty, press her thumb to her chest, with a clentched fist, and immediately say, "I'm going to do it."

Add to this, her love for elevator floor button pushing in the fifty-seven-story apartment building we lived in at the time. Other building residents quickly learned, don't even think about going near the floor button panel when Olivia was present. She had to push it. She insisted on pushing it. You make the mistake and push it by accident and habit? Not a good ride up, or down, for anyone.

There was an incident in Water Tower Place, a mall on Michigan Avenue just across the street from our apartment. Both kids would go there to play, as many city kids do. Anya, our nanny at the time, took Olivia to the public bathroom. These bathrooms had been recently renovated. Unbeknownst to Anya, this new potty had an automatic flusher. Anya told us later that Olivia threw a major wing ding when she got off the potty and it flushed. She assumed Anya flushed the toilet, which was forbidden. Anya tells us her outburst was so loud and long that security was called as a result of a report from a woman in the bathroom who must have assumed Olivia was being kidnapped, given her ear-piercing screams and behavior. Anya got out safely, but Olivia wouldn't let it go. At least once or twice each day, for at least a month after the incident, she would rev up and repeat, "Anya flushed the toilet."

Pushing the button. Flushing the toilet. She had to be the one to take action and be in charge.

Perseverance

Another character trait was revealed when she was around three. Ellen's parents, Toni and Stuart, who were a huge help raising both kids, enjoyed puzzles. So did I as a fat child, while eating chips and licorice. We frequently had one in progress on the glass dining room table. This one in particular was very hard. It featured a large blue sky.

Olivia was sitting on her Aunt Amy's lap. Amy, Ellen's older sister, was another huge help in raising the kids, who then called her, "Aunty Matey." Olivia was determined to work on the puzzle. She always wanted to be with the adults, and clearly is getting frustrated and the hissing is about to start. After about twenty minutes of encouragement from all to keep at it, "persevere," an important Karas verb I taught both kids early on, she succeeds. The single piece she's been working with finally fits. She starts to uncontrollably cry, "I did it. I did it. I got a piece." That's why I ended the last chapter with she "did it" in quotes. She sobs for at least two to three minutes.

Olivia was going to do it, regardless of how long and painful the process. None of us really thought about this fact until much later when she had found her sport and demonstrated this same drive and determination to succeed.

> *NOTE:* My first book, *The Business Plan for the Body*, came out in spring 2001. It was about weight loss. Each chapter began with a quote. The final chapter was about what do you do now that you have successfully lost weight? What was the quote for the chapter? "I did it. I did it," attributed to Olivia, who just turned four when the book came out. I don't think she truly knows what an impact she has always had on me. Even as a child she inspired me and continues to inspire me. I thought, *If she can maneuver a "vehicle" out of a corner before her first year and find the right fit for her piece of the sky, she "did it" by the age of three, then I should be able to write a book at thirty-nine.*

Fearlessness

Olivia starts half day, junior kindergarten at Chicago City Day. Mrs. Wilson, a wonderful woman who has since retired, was her teacher. One of the first mornings, all the kids went outside for recess. Typical. They were four. How much of an attention span do you have at that age? Ellen receives a totally panicky phone call from Mrs. Wilson, who is out of breath.

"Ellen, I'm so sorry to bother you but we have a major issue with Olivia."

"What, what is it? Is she alright?"

"Yes, but we can't get her down from the high money bars on the playground. She refuses. She's not even listening. Other classmates are trying to climb up with her."

"Oh, she does crazy stuff like that all the time. She has no fear. She will be fine. Just get the others down so they don't get hurt."

The Addiction

By the time she was six and in first grade, Olivia had a pretty typical city schedule of after-school activities, such as:

Monday—skating
Tuesday—gymnastics
Wednesday—Brownies
Thursday—ballet
Friday—art class

Her gymnastics teacher, Olga speaks to Ellen after one class and asks if Olivia would be willing to come to the gym not once, but twice a week. We didn't know why. I guess she saw potential.

We sit Olivia down in the living room and explain, "Your gymnastics teacher would like you to come a second time each week. Are you up for it?"

Without missing a beat, "YES!"

Before we knew it, she was at the gym twenty-three hours a week, which I previously referenced. She was a crack addict, and her "crack" was gymnastics. Immediately our lives revolved around her sport. Until Olivia was nine, Ellen and I were still married, and I was commuting to New York for work, Monday through Friday, at least forty-five weeks a year. Ellen was still rehearsing and performing, mostly out of town, around six months a year. We had full-time help, and at one point, we had to have two helpers because we needed the extra set of hands seven days a week. Olivia's schedule required air traffic control between us, Ellen's parents, Amy, other gymnastics parents, one or two full-time helpers, Kristen, my assistant at the time, a great cab driver named Mike Cade who would take her from school and to the gym and often back home from the gym (this is pre-Uber), and so on. It dictated a good portion of our lives.

Once we got divorced in 2006, we moved into apartment buildings right next door to each other. Both buildings shared the same building manager, building manager's office, and receiving room. From the front, it actually appears to be the same building. The kids could freely take the elevator or stairs to our respective apartments. We alternated weeks with the kids and kept the full-time help. I would shorten my New York trip when it was my week with the kids, and when Ellen was working out of town, the kids stayed full time with me because they were in school. Then Ellen retired from acting when Olivia was eleven and the back-and-forth weeks were somewhat easier. We just made it work, but again, with the help of a lot of extra, loving hands.

Parent tip: This was our "new normal," and just about everything revolved around her schedule. If your child wishes to pursue any high-level sport, your "new normal" may look something like ours.

Looking back, no one minded. No one complained. She was moving. She loved training. She was happy.

What's more important than that?

Chapter 4
LET THE GAMES BEGIN!

CONFESSION—*Certain "moves" moved me.*

From November until late spring, my Saturdays were devoted to club gymnastic competitions. This is important to note. Unlike most student athletes, Olivia's sport didn't take place at school. She went to a gym we paid for her to attend, like a club. Many of you reading may be in a sport at school or be the parent of an athlete. Sure, there are some costs, such as uniforms, certain equipment, and maybe outside training or coaching. But in the club world of gymnastics, it doesn't happen without the dollars.

For those of you fortunate enough (I hope you feel the irony in my use of the word "fortunate") to attend club gymnastic competitions, it's really a four-ring circus because all four apparatus are going at the same time. You know when your team is up on which apparatus and sometimes have to move seats to get a better view, depending on the layout of the competition arena. These meets are L O N G because some clubs have huge teams. And the big teams generally had the mediocre competitors since the coaches could not give much individual attention.

Let's let Olivia explain:

Club-Level Competitions

Club levels have changed in recent years, but this is how it was during my tenure. The lowest level for competing is Level 4. This is the base of all things gymnastics. Level 4 is also called a compulsory level, which essentially means the routines are created by USA Gymnastics (USAG) and then performed *exactly* the same by every athlete competing in that level. Levels 4–6 were all compulsory levels during my club days, so they had the same rules, the exact same routine for each event and for floor, and the exact same music. They have just recently changed the levels, but I don't even know what the new reasoning is for that change. Bottom line, everyone did the same thing on every single event through Level 6.

Levels 7–10 were the optional levels where athletes were given set requirements to be completed in the routine, but the choreography, music, preferred skills, and originality were all up to the athlete and her coach. These years offered much more creativity and comfort because you had the chance to choose what you felt you did best, then perform it.

My first competition was when I was seven years old. Olga didn't want me competing in the lowest level at the time, Level 4, as she felt I could skip it. Instead, she wanted me to focus on the skills needed to begin my career competing at Level 5 with girls much older than me.

A Surprise Performance

JIM INTERJECTION: One, early competition in Level 6 has always stayed with me. It was somewhere in Illinois since Olivia never competed outside the state until Level 8. For this meet, we are seated not in the brutal, hard bleachers but instead in elevated, makeshift theater chairs, and they are far more raised and pitched. Actually, it was like a theater balcony, but we were very close and looking slightly down at the girls. You could really see the competitors. This was a very well attended, long competition, and oddly, every other team has finished their rotation. Olivia is the only person left to compete, and it's floor, clearly her first love. She just lit up whenever she heard her music begin.

As mentioned in Level 6, *all* competitors perform the same floor routine to the same music. Many of us who endured Level 6 meets agree, we still suffer a mild post-traumatic stress disorder from listening to the same song, over and over again and watching the same routine, over and over again.

Right from the start, Olivia took competing *very* seriously. Add to that a strict Eastern European coach, and you can imagine why she doesn't just walk on the floor to strike her beginning pose. Instead, she does a very specific military-ish strut to hit her opening stance. You might recall that Olga Korbut, the darling of the Munich Olympics, did that as well. Has to be the Russian influence.

Olivia does her strut and strikes her opening stance, always a very dramatic pose with emotion. I thought nothing of it, as she's done this routine many times before. All this attention won't get to her. Wrong. It did. I could see her eyes cheat over to the audience as her music started. She must have felt all the eyes on her. It amped her up, and her performance was *big*. At one point, she is supposed to drop down to the floor, then get right back up. Olivia dramatically throws herself onto the floor, then pops up tall and proud, with perfect posture and attitude. Her pigtails were flying high, given the magnitude of this grand movement. The audience gasped. I gasped as I had never quite seen this level of performance from her before. At the end of her routine when she hit her final, dramatic pose, the audience actually applauded, which really isn't done at these types of competitions. She rapidly exits the floor and runs and hugs Olga. Clay, a fellow teammate's dad, leans over and says to me, "No one should every do that routine again after Olivia's performance."

Olivia interjection: I don't remember this at all—nothing.

I Didn't Think About Winning

To be honest, I didn't think about winning often. I always wanted to do my absolute best but rarely thought about winning. In fact, the only time I ever consciously thought, *I want to win* was at my first state championships in Level 6 where the best gymnast in her respective level earns the title of state champion. Now, I didn't want the title, but I wanted the t-shirt they awarded the winners that had their name on the back, showing their victory. I don't think I have ever actually told anyone this fact. Oh, I got the t-shirt.

My Early Recollections

So, to be clear, I don't remember competing in Level 5 or 6. I don't remember dad's story about competing last on floor. I do remember *wanting* the t-shirt at the state championship, but what I did that day to win first? No clue. *My* earliest recollection of competing in club was my first Level 7 meet, now in optional gymnastics. I distinctly recall stepping out on the floor to begin my floor routine, amped up to debut it. Olga and I worked hard on choosing the right music to the right moves. I loved it

Confessions of a **DIVISION-I ATHLETE**

and couldn't wait to show it off. My small pale legs were shaking with excitement to perform my new, personalized routine. I slowly configured into my beginning pose, waiting to hear the loud beep at the beginning of my music to signal the start. The beep echoed through the small, smelly (that I remember) gymnasium, and I counted down a second and a half before I began dancing to my music once it started. Only seconds after it began, it abruptly stopped.

I kept dancing, so engrossed in my performance, until I realized I was dancing to silence. I slowly began fading out of my performance, lifting my eyes to Olga as if to look for a solution. Olga mouthed to me, "Keep going," which I didn't register. Finally, I recall looking at the judges' table, hoping they would tell me to step off the floor and start over.

"Keep going!" the judge said. I stood there frozen. "Keeeeeeeeeeeppppp gooooooooinnnggggggg" she said slowly and loudly, as if to make it register with me. Realizing I had no choice but to continue, I finished the routine to the tempo of the audience, my teammates, and other fellow competitors clapping.

As I finished my routine, thrilled with my execution given the adversity, Olga rushed over.

"Olivusa," she said (that's what she frequently called me), "The judge said you can go again at end of rotation. Do you want?"

Was I ever going to turn down an opportunity to perform *again?*
"YES!"

I competed once more at the end, doing an equally fine routine. But it wasn't the score or the routine; it was the chance to perform yet again. I lived for it.

Someone actually filmed my second floor routine at this meet and posted it on YouTube. I guess they saw the first routine done to claps and were excited to see it done to the music. Apparently, it got upwards of 100,000 hits until someone told me it was taken down a few years later. Regardless, it was so cool to think that someone noticed my performance.

My First Regional Meet

I was twelve when I competed in my first Level 8 Regional competition. This is the farthest you can go in Level 8. Level 8 Regionals is the first time you compete against a pool of athletes beyond just your state. I was assigned to Region 5, which consisted of gymnasts who lived in Illinois, Indiana, Kentucky, Michigan, and Ohio. Level 9 takes it beyond just the regions and is the first season where half the nation competes against each other. These meets are Easterns and Westerns. Finally, Level 10 is when the whole nation comes together to compete, and the true best of the nation is crowned. Level 10 is also what all collegiate gymnasts compete at throughout college. Elite is different, which I will explain later.

JIM INTERJECTION: Her first, Level 8 regional competition was held in Findlay, Ohio (a hot spot!). Olivia was twelve years old and was doing well. I was a little shocked because I assumed at this level and at Regionals, all the girls would have similar skills. Not true. Sure, there were some stand-outs, but at this meet it was obvious to me that Olivia was, well, a bit of a wow.

There was another talented gymnast at this meet from another Illinois gym. Olivia and she had competed against each other before. She was good, right on Olivia's heels. Her name is Ally Hoyer. Their scores were neck and neck. FYI—they continued to compete against each other in college as Ally got a full ride to Michigan State. And, for those of you who don't know about Michigan, these two schools are big rivals.

I really tried to not be score-centric (I don't know if that is a word or if I made it up). I wanted my energy to be focused on Olivia and not on the scores or the other girls. I also never cheered or made a sound while Olivia was competing. I'm weird but do believe our kids feel and pick up on our energy. I always wanted it to be positive. But being an economics major, again the son of an accountant (we only discussed numbers at the infrequent, unpleasant, family dinner table), I can total up numbers pretty fast. I never monitored her scores while she was competing. I only paid attention once I somewhat understood how it worked and how they determined who took first, second, third, and lower. We move to the awards area. Frequently you had to move from the competition floor to another area for awards.

Awards ceremonies are in Olympic order, and it's always the same: vault, bars, beam, then floor. Those are the four events or apparatus, and at this young age, pretty much everyone does all four. After the individual medals are given out, it ends with the "all-around" award to the competitor who had the highest cumulative score on all four events. Then they would finally award the all-around team.

Olivia and Ally take turns on the podiums as the ceremony begins. They are sharing first and second place, back and forth, always by a slight margin.

I didn't know the awards and medals for a regional competition. This was my first one. I knew there was ultimately an all-around winner but assumed it wasn't a big deal, as it hadn't been before.

I'm adding, and I remember what Olivia got on floor and realize, oh my God, I think Olivia won the all-around.

They start out in tenth or twelfth place (don't get me started about why anyone needs to be recognized for twelfth place, millennials!) and progress until they get to third, second, and finally, first.

They call her name, and as she is climbing up the lower podiums to go to the first place "all-around" top position, she stops and hugs Ally, who is standing on the second-place position. I was actually more *moved* by this *move* than any of the *moves* she executed during the meet.

This continued throughout her career. Sometimes, given the same scores, winners would share a podium with others. Olivia was lucky enough to frequently be on the top. During her club years, you didn't know who would take first place all-around as there were *so* many competitors and almost never was a computer or electronic scoreboard used to post the scores. During her Michigan years, it was different because during season, 75 percent of the time it was just two teams competing, so you watched each and every routine. The two-team competition also made watching it on the live stream, the Big Ten Network, or ESPN feel as if you were there. The other 25 percent of the time, it was three, four, or even six teams competing. We will explain how that works later on.

During her four years at Michigan, the girls knew in advance who was taking certain positions because everything was up on the Jumbotron, updated constantly. If Olivia received a 9.95 on floor and you didn't see another score that high or higher from another gymnast, you knew she would be taking first place on the event. Therefore, they also knew who would ultimately take the individual all-around and then the team all-around title.

During these college meets, if Olivia's name was called first for the number one position, she would wait until the second or sometimes third competitor was called and walk up together to share the podium. Again, she would know in advance if there was a tie. If it was a fellow Michigan teammate, they held hands, which happened a lot with freshman Natalie Wojcik during Olivia's senior year. I always thought, *Such a lady. So respectful of the other girls. She didn't get that from me. I would have run up to the top spot, assumed the "warrior" position with feet spread and hands on hips and let the other girls struggle to stay on the back corner of the small podium for dear life, even if it was my own teammate*. Sometimes the apple does fall far, sometimes very far, from the tree!

Now to be clear, there were some "not so polite" teams and "not so polite" individuals. I am forbidden from mentioning a few of the "rude" teams and the "rude" fans of the teams in the stadium. This mostly happened out of town. Olivia and her team *always* cheered for their competitors. As proud as I was and still am with regard to how Olivia excelled at her sport, I am equally proud of how she conducted herself in each and every competition. No attitude. No bad behavior. Except for a couple of falls, which happens to everyone at some point, she kept her energy positive on the outside.

Olivia interjection: The last thing you want to do as an athlete is show blatant disappointment. After all, you are competing in front of an audience filled with family, friends, other competitors' families, and sometimes even a fan or two. Their perception of you comes from far more than just your gymnastics. It has to do with your attitude. People tend to shy away from rooting for the little brat who throws a tantrum when she falls off beam. At the end of the day, the name of the game of gymnastics is to make it look easy and effortless. You want to remain "poised" (more on that word later) to the best of your ability and sulk about it later on. Otherwise, it'll just make getting back up even harder than it already is.

Competition Hair

For all competitions, Olivia had to have pigtails, very specific pigtails. No crooked part or flyaway hairs in the back hanging down, only tight, symmetrical pigtails.

Ellen mostly did them, but when she was away rehearsing or performing, others had to do them, and when they weren't perfect, Olivia would regress to her "vehicle" pushing, corner hissing phase.

Below is a list of pigtail, meltdown victims:

- Her sweet grandmother, Toni, who tied up the tails with mismatched ponytail holders. She is also an impressive seamstress who tailored the kids' clothes beautifully. She knows how to create a straight line, but alas, not always as straight as Olivia thought they should be.
- My good friend Jana, who apparently produced asymmetric pigtails at an Indianapolis meet, off by maybe one centimeter.
- Ellen, though she knew how to shut it down and put Olivia in her place.
- Evan, because he pulled one of her pigtails and knocked it out of place.
- Aunt Amy, who has a BA in mechanical engineering and an MBA. Even she could not always manage the approved "tails."

- Me. I tried. I would say I had a 50 percent success rate. The flyaway hairs in the back always were my nemesis, and early on, she figured how to manipulate my three-way bathroom mirrors to see the back. It wasn't pretty . . .

Our eardrums, nerves, and tolerance for pigtail symmetry are gone but never forgotten.

I never knew why she choose pigtails for competition, so as we are writing this chapter, I asked:

"What was with the pigtails? You were obsessed with them from your first Level 5 competition when you were seven years old until you turned thirteen and were about to compete in Level 9.

"Dad, do you remember Olga Korbut? She was my idol when I was younger. She wore pigtails. I wanted to be her, so I made pigtails my signature look."

"Why did you abruptly make a switch? I remember one day they were gone."

"DAD, I've told you, and you never listen. Olga met her at a competition, and she said she was possibly the meanest person she had ever met, and so my fandom ended. Pigtails out, pony in.

Aren't You Olivia's Dad?

During a Level 9 competition, I vividly remember waiting in the concession stand line in Bourbonnais, Illinois (another hot spot!), before a competition. For the record, I drank a ton of iced tea to stay awake, and it has amazing health benefits. I couldn't keep myself from not giving any healthy advice. Me bad. I would chug my tea and eat a big, doughy, salted pretzel. I know—carbs—but trust me, it was the best option when the other alternatives were hot dogs and nachos. One of the fathers standing next to me said, "Aren't you Olivia's dad? You know, there really are two competitions here today. All the other girls and then whether Olivia will get a higher all-around score from last week." I was shocked, not only by the comments, but more so because I started to realize people were taking note of my daughter.

We shared these specific stories because I believe they illustrate the qualities Olivia began to nurture and grow as her career progressed.

Athletic ability? Totally from her mom. Ellen is very well known in the theatre world as an actor who did a great deal of physical comedy, some that involved throwing her around the stage.

Performing? Both Ellen and I are performers, so Olivia got a double dose of that.

Competitive nature? The crazy, teeth gritting competitor comes from me. It's just part of who I am and what motivates me. I don't fight it. Nor does she. We both embrace it.

Olivia had the formula:

> Athletic Ability +
>   Joy of Performing +
>   Strong Competitive Spirit =
>   Success

That was her winning trifecta.

Olivia interjection: I knew that the difficulty and skills were only part of it. At the end of the day, it came down to what set me apart as a young athlete from the other competitors. I firmly believe it was my honest love for the sport. Having all three of those things is important to any competitor in any sport. You have to have the skill, then enjoy showing what you can do in front of people and finally being competitive with a goal to be your best.

As I neared the end of my gymnastics career, I realized my assigned percentages for this trifecta:

Athletic Ability—40 percent, then build on that ability through consistent practice and relentlessly rehabbing your injuries.

Competitive Grit—20 percent, the love of pressure, fight and dedication to your sport.

Joy of Performing—40 percent, go out and have fun and share your joy. This was truly my favorite.

I had the ability. Plus, for the most part, I had excellent coaching, both mentally and physically.

Competing and I generally got along well. Outside of some "beam blues," I loved it.

Performing. Boy, what a rush! This is going to be a hard one to replace in the next chapter of my life.

When all three percentages were at full force, I felt invincible.

Chapter 5
THE FIRST "SECOND" MOTHER

CONFESSION—*We fought and loved like mother and daughter.*

I was fortunate in my career to have only a few coaches. In club, I started at one gym with Olga and followed her when she opened her own. There are girls who we refer to as "gym hoppers," essentially girls who can't stay at one gym for more than a couple years, probably because they blame the gym or coach, or both, instead of relying on their own ability. They hop from one gym to another, sometimes numerous times. I am proud to say that 95 percent of the girls at my gym were home grown and never left to go elsewhere. We were all loyal to our coach and subconsciously looked down on the "gym hoppers" for their lack of faith and belief.

Our loyalty showed. Each and every one of us was trained to display elegance, flexibility, and power. We were also taught to strive for a high level of performance, which many other teams simply did not emphasize. Our Eastern European coaches had a very specific style and protocol. We had to take ballet twice a week, which we *hated*. Every time I complained, my dad would point out, "Look, ballet is teaching you how to precisely finish each move. That's why your team stands out amongst the other girls." Still, doesn't change the fact that every Tuesday and Thursday from 4:30–5:30, we wanted to die.

I met Olga when I was six years old. I've never told anyone this, but the first time I ever practiced with her as my coach, I felt an instant connection. I somehow knew she would take me somewhere, and I didn't even know where "somewhere" was going to be.

When I tell you coaches become second parents, I'm not talking about a parent who frequently picks you up from school for a play date with your best friend. I'm talking about someone who more times than not feeds you, knows your biggest fears and roadblocks, knows how to tell you to get your shit together when you're being lazy, and frankly, just knows you more than you and sometimes your parents do.

It became evident Olga was a second mother to me very early on. Most of this may have to do with this fact: I was usually by myself at meets. Club gymnastics is organized by age groups. Girls who may be in the same grade academically may be placed in separate age groups according to when their birthday falls. This is due to the high volume of girls in the sport. It just happened I spent a lot of time competing alone with just Olga and her daughter, who was the assistant coach, at my side. By age twelve, I also started leaving school early on Tuesdays and Thursdays to attend more focused training with her and two other girls. I began to progress much quicker than even she expected. I didn't understand that at the time, but I can clearly see that now.

I distinctly remember a moment at Level 9 Eastern Nationals at the Charleston Civic Center in Charleston, West Virginia. It was on my thirteenth birthday, April 30, 2010. As mentioned, Level 9 splits Nationals into two competitions, Eastern and Western. It's a big deal because it is the first time that you get to compete at a national level against girls outside of the Midwest. I now understand it, which I didn't at the time. I just knew this meet was a BFD.

Lucky me, we start on beam. Later on, I will devote not one, but two chapters on my nemesis, the beam. To give you a little taste of what is to come, in classic Olivia Karas fashion, I manage to stay on the beam for my routine yet slip on my dismount and face plant—at Eastern Nationals. I'm looking at the mat, with my nose touching it, when I *should* be saluting on my feet immediately after my intended "stuck" dismount. I was thirteen and very much the beam's bitch, which is my opening confession of chapter 9.

The gritty, competitive Jim Karas in me was not about to spend my birthday sulking because I fell on beam. At that age, birthdays were the best days of the year because they're all about you. Although I am "Christmas crazy," I still have quite a soft spot for April 30. My thirteenth birthday was no exception. I remember thinking, "No way am I marking this day with the beam blunder. Wait. Floor is next. This is my chance for redemption."

At this point in my career, my parents still lacked a lot of knowledge about the specifics of the sport and the scoring. I liked that. Sure, my dad could add, but that's it. Evan actually figured out the scoring and all of the rules by the time he was eight and I was twelve. He's annoyingly smart. Everyone else had absolutely no idea what was going on. They followed the simple gymnastics rules:

Fall = Bad
Stay On = Good
Stick the Landing = Really Good

Regardless of whether I fell, stayed on, or stuck the landing on any apparatus, my family applauded and smiled because they knew I loved it.

Fact: I actually don't recall a specific moment where I realized that floor was my favorite event. I just know my thought process went like this:

Vault: Run full speed toward a stationary object. Can't dance. No music. No originality. Nope.

Bars: Unnatural for me as my body is made more like Mary Lou Retton's—powerful. Hurt my shoulders. Mentally and physically was the most difficult for me. No music. No originality. Nope.

Beam: No way—keep reading.

Floor: Originality. Music. Performing. Fun. Dancing—Yep!

Back to my birthday: I remember waiting to go on floor and smiling because I was about to compete in my favorite event on this special day. When the judge's arm went up to signal me to begin, I smiled even more. Get ready, here comes a full-blown floor routine, complete with birthday steroids.

My dad was unable to make it to this meet. He made such an effort to always be there, but sometimes, reading the *Wall Street Journal* (he will explain later) at a gymnastics meet in the middle of a cornfield didn't work with his busy schedule. He had what he calls a "Big Boy" speech out of town that conflicted. We were going to celebrate my birthday the next day. I understood and was totally okay with it. I looked up into the crowd to see my mom smiling and applauding, Evan, wearing a hat with a spinning propeller on top clapping, and my grandparents (so very special to me) smiling and waving at me. I also knew my dad had his phone in hand ready to hear from my mom after I finished each routine. Remember the Karas verb, "persevere?" I heard him in my head saying, "Come on, Pokey (my nickname based off of Pokémon), persevere."

I finished my routine, a good one I can honestly say, and ran over to give Olga the biggest hug.

A fellow region five coach came over to us as I began hugging the other girls on my team and tapped Olga. I heard her ask, "I have always wondered—is Olivia your daughter?"

Olga laughed and pointed to her daughter standing next to her, acknowledging she was her actual daughter. She then pointed up into the stands and told the coach, "That's Olivia's mother!" and my mom was smiling and clapping. Olga always made sure people knew who my actual mom was.

Once the meet was over, and my post-beam blues had diminished, it was time for the award ceremony.

I received the best birthday present: I won the Eastern National Floor Title. I stood up on the first-place podium, smiling ear to ear with a big mouth stuffed with braces and received my first big gold medal. When the medal was around my neck, I looked down and saw my mom and Olga with their arms around each other. They yelled "Happy Birthday!" as loudly as they could. What a day—perseverance after a fall, my first gold medal, and realizing how lucky I was to have not one, but two important "moms" in my life. Different women, different upbringings and perspectives, but both had my back and their arms around each other. Happy Birthday! A "win," but not just because of the medal. Much more so because I started to understand that I had a lot of support.

Let me be clear, though. Olga and I didn't only get along. We loved like second mother and daughter and fought like second mother and daughter, especially when it came to how many of each routine or skill I had to do at practice. When I was younger and pre-pubescent, I thought doing more was fun. I welcomed it. But as I got older, and endured more injuries, it all began to hurt. The pain led to me not wanting to do it, which led to an argument.

Olga was stubborn. I was stubborn. We both very firmly stuck to our opinions. As I got older and more mature and believed in my way versus her way, we constantly clashed. It's not like I thought I knew everything. I just felt I knew what was best for me.

She believed in me. She wanted me to become an Olympian. She thought I could do it. After all, it is supposed to be every competitor's dream. But it wasn't mine. I just didn't want to do it.

JIM INTERJECTION: For those not aware of the gymnastics world, you have to make a decision to take one of two paths:

1. The Olympic or elite path. The elite program is specifically designed for athletes who will represent the United States at international competitions, such as

the Olympics and the World Championship, to name a few. These athletes attend regional and national training programs specifically designed for them and their very specific end goal. They also compete in annual elite competitions, such as the American Cup, the US championships and the US classic. You can't simply say you are an elite. In order to get to compete at this level, a gymnast must pass both the elite compulsory and optional qualifiers.

According to USA Gymnastics, at any time there are between thirty and eighty women in the elite program. For the upcoming 2021 summer Olympics, only four female gymnasts will represent the United States. Years ago, there were seven, then six, and then five. Now only four. Why, you may ask? Right now, we are not quite sure, but a lot of women must be upset that so few will have this amazing opportunity. Of the four, only two will compete "all-around" and the other two, only a few of the individual apparatus.

Elite training necessitates six hours of training a day, six days a week. This is the path Olga chose during her years of competing—thirty-six hours a week compared to Olivia's already grueling twenty-three. While on the Olympic path, you don't go to school. You are home schooled or do an online school, which is what Olivia did. It's brutal. It's depressing watching your child sit on his or her bed or at your kitchen table on their computer by themselves. Olivia did it for five months and bailed. Stay tuned for why.

2. The collegiate path. According to USA Gymnastics, there are at least 1,000 women competing at Level 10, which is the highest level before elite and what all collegiate gymnasts compete at. This is for those who are looking for a university or collegiate scholarship or looking to "walk on," which again, means being accepted on the team but offered no scholarship money at the time. That can change in the future depending on circumstances such as a gymnast leaving the school or having to "medically retire" due to injury. If you do retire due to an injury, you give the athletic scholarship back to the team but do have your entire tuition, room and board paid for by a seperate fund. There is not cost to an athlete to medically retire. Events such as these and others could therefore open up a full or partial scholarship. On this path, the *team*, as you will learn, is far more important than you as an individual competitor.

My inner "Sherlock Holmes" is coming out as I was googling the difference in cost between Level 10 and elite.

I would estimate that throughout Olivia's club years as a competitor, I was easily spending close to $10,000 to $15,000 a year, some years more because the addition of regional and national meets.

"Mandatory" costs would include team dues to Olga's gym (a big portion of that amount) for her team group practice sessions, meet fees, practice leotards, competition leotards (which could easily cost hundreds of dollars depending on the level of "bling," grips (used for bars), tape, travel back and forth from the gym whether it was in the form of gas, a taxi or Uber, and so on, and this was just for Olivia.

Optional costs may include private training hours with the coach (I did this for Olivia and Olga), co-pays for the numerous visits to the doctor for injuries and then the out-of-pocket expenses for the numerous treatments. Some experimental procedures were completely out of pocket, as many cutting-edge treatments have yet to receive federal approval. Now, if you wish to attend these meets, add gas, meet admissions fees for family and friends (I felt it was my responsibility to pay for anyone willing to drive that far and sit that long), air travel when required, and this was for Olivia, Evan, Ellen, and me. Hotels, food, taxis or Uber, I don't know if I ever really looked at the cost, but it was significant.

Elite training, for some, can cost upwards of six figures. That is on the high end. It is a huge financial obligation, so if you are considering this route, know what you are getting into.

But, the businessman in me must also point out, there are two potential outcomes, depending on the collegiate versus elite path:

1. Olivia had a full ride at Michigan. I virtually had *no* out-of-pocket expenses. Given I would have paid out-of-state tuition, the total with tuition, room and board was approximately $65,000. For four years, that saved me $260,000. According to my research:
   □ Division-I schools are permitted twelve scholarships for their women's gymnastics program. Division I is what the NCAA calls a head-count sport and the

total number of athletes receiving money cannot exceed twelve. There are sixty D-I gymnastics teams in the NCAA. If each provides twelve (and some may not due to a lack of funds, so check) there could be a maximum of 720 scholarships.

◦ Division-II schools are permitted six scholarships for their women's gymnastics program. But, D-II gymnastics teams are not held to the head-count rule, so they could, for instance, provide twelve athletes a 50 percent scholarship or eighteen athletes on one-third scholarship if they chose to do so. There are six D-II gymnastics teams in the NCAA.

◦ Division-III schools do not offer athletic scholarships. There are fourteen D-III gymnastics teams.

NOTE: Division I teams in the Ivy League are not permitted to offer athletic scholarships. But they and other schools who don't have athletic scholarship funds are permitted to provide need-based financial aid on a case-by-case basis per family in the form of financial grants.

As an elite gymnast, here is the amount you won at the 2016 Olympics:

    a. Gold—$37,500
    b. Silver—$22,500
    c. Bronze—$15,000

But endorsement money may ultimately come with multiple millions of dollars. Depending on the success of the endorsement, this may be a multi-year opportunity, and not just a short-lived financial windfall.

ADDITIONAL NOTE: NCAA athletes in the future can receive endorsement money while competing in an amateur status for their school. Prior to that, endorsement money, while attending and competing for your school, was not allowed. California first changed the state law, then ultimately, and pretty quickly, it was changed throughout the entire country by the NCAA. The details of exactly when and how this will be allowed is still being conceptualized, so stay tuned.

As she was about to bail on the elite path in December 2014, Olivia looks at me with her wide eyes, and points her finger at me for the first time as I explained she would about a year later when she declared, "I want them to want me just as much as I want them." She says, "Look, I know what you want (yes, I wanted her in the Olympics), but it's not what I want. You need to accept my decision. I want to be on a team!"

To be clear, the Olympic team is a "team" only once, for the team all-around competition. After that, it's every woman for herself. It quickly becomes a one-man or in this instance, one-woman show. I'm sure I'm going to get nasty tweets or comments from former Olympians, but it's simply the truth. Once the team all-around competition is over, look out, as your "teammate" is now your "team not," as she has joined all the other competitors.

At Michigan, it's always about the team. You are one important part and have the responsibility to score as high as possible for the team. Olivia could never be truly happy if she did well at a meet but her team did not. It was all about the team's success.

Begrudgingly, I did listen to Olivia and supported her taking the collegiate route. It was the right direction mentally (the stress was off the charts) and absolutely the right decision physically. I don't believe her body would have tolerated the required volume of training hours. Yes, it was the right decision, but I had a vision of her on that Rio podium and then on the Wheaties box.

With every partnership comes battles. I firmly believe Olga and I battled because we cared, but we sure did battle.

Another reason we clashed was from a very early age, I had a strong commitment to doing things myself. My dad already told you about the toilet flushing and elevator button pushing, so this should come as no surprise. I also had to do it right. I hated being given negative feedback. In fact, whenever I messed up and was given a correction, I got even more upset. I wanted to be perfect as my sport required it. I knew I messed up. I didn't need to be told.

For instance, vault and bars are far more technical than beam and floor. Although a vault is only six seconds, so much happens, so quickly, that in order to train correctly, you have to break the vault down. So, when I would mess up doing a drill for vault or the vault itself, and I was told I messed up, I got mad. Like, "no sh&t" I messed up. Frequently, I fell on my face.

When I was eight, I so badly wanted to compete in Level 6, as it required a back flip on floor. I wasn't done with Level 5 yet and was already begging Olga to let me try the back flip. She refused, as we were mid-season in Level 5, and I didn't like that answer. So instead, I stayed late one day when she was working with the older girls, and with numerous attempts, I taught myself, proving that I could do it "all on my own!"

When I stopped the elite path in January 2014 and went back to Level 10 club gymnastics, we had a better relationship. I once again realized she was in my corner. She realized I had made the decision and was going to Michigan. I finally asked for help and welcomed her coaching. As you will learn in chapter 11, this shift also took my club career to the next level.

Chapter 6
"I WISH YOU WERE NEVER BORN"

CONFESSION—*I had to apologize.*

Well, this may come as no surprise, especially to those of you who have either had a coach; had a sibling, friend, or family member experience a coach; or are the parent of a child who presently has a coach. It's often-times not good. Every coach's business is built on their best talent. Olivia was the machine that drove a huge amount of business to Olga's gym. Olga knew it. I knew it. Olivia didn't know it.

As to *not* open myself up for slander, or libel, or whatever someone can sue you for, I want you to always begin each of the subsequent paragraphs with the word "allegedly." But it's all true.

Olga was always a rough ride. It was her way or the highway. I know, this sounds a lot like Olivia. It also sounds like me. I actually didn't know at the time that Olivia and Olga clashed as much as she has since shared. It makes perfect sense now. Olivia *always* protected Olga, and I was the "bad guy" when I would go on an Olga rant. Now, she did groom my daughter into a beautiful athlete. As I said, you can actually tell which gymnasts, even at the collegiate level, were trained by an Eastern European coach. There is an elegance that is evident in the presentational skills and the completion of each move. Every toe is pointed, every hand is held in a certain way, posture, and attitude before, during, and after a routine. There is also emotion. You perform your routine. You don't just go through the motions. It's quite exceptional. Olga has a great eye for talent. Her ability to help those with exceptional skill reach the top levels of their talent is noted. She has played a big role in Olivia's career and in her life. For this, I will say, "thank you."

Olga was not happy at the gym she was working for, which was about 2.5 miles from our home in the city. It was easy to take Olivia there and easy to pick her up or have her picked up. I bring up this geographical issue because it soon will become a critical one.

We began to hear rumblings of some sort of disfavor. The owner of this gym favored the boys' gymnastics team and the boys' coach over Olga. She told this to the girls, and it filtered to the parents. Looking back, I'm sure this was the first step of her "master" plan. Again, the club gym business is big business. Olga wanted to move from employee to owner.

One of the mothers—let's call her "Roberta"—started to explore other options in the city, as her daughter was also on the team. I heard about a possible move, thankfully within the city.

Yada, yada, yada, Roberta comes up with a business plan and is going to be some kind of partner or whatever with this new venture. I get the phone call. "Jim, as Olivia is clearly a leader on the team, all the parents are wondering how much you are willing to invest?" This "investment" comes with an approximately 10 percent interest rate, which means you are going to get, on a yearly basis until she pays us back, ten dollars of interest for every hundred dollars invested.

While 10 percent is nothing to scoff at, I never thought there was a chance in hell I would see this money again. We hear Olga's husband really wants to move to Florida (something Olivia did not know until she went to Michigan). If she was going to leave this current situation, the only way Olga was staying was to have her own gym.

I believe the total raise was something around $350,000 to $400,000. I'm not totally sure and certainly won't be calling Roberta or Olga to "fact check."

Confessions of a **DIVISION-I ATHLETE**

I say to Roberta, "I will put in $10,000." This investment is crazy risky as Olga has no track record of owning and operating a gym. I also don't know what Roberta's reason was for participating, nor do I know if she has any experience in this capacity. Maybe she was bored.

Current owner gets wind that Olga is building a competitive gym and tosses her and the girls out. They have to train in temporary quarters, which is just south of our home but still in the city. Not a great commute, but not as bad as the suburbs.

Let me digress—If Olga didn't get her own gym, we would be schlepping Olivia about thirty miles west of the city, in traffic, six days a week, easily an hour to an hour and a half each way. Impossible. A nightmare. I had to do whatever I could to make my life, and all our lives, easier with a city gym. Plus, Olivia loved Olga.

Once again, "it's happening." The deal is almost done, and they are ready to close on the new venture. At the eleventh hour, I get a somewhat panicky call from Roberta.

"Jim, we are short and are looking for another $50,000 for the new gym. What are you willing to do as Olga has told us (again, as "persuasion" knowing the city parents didn't want her to go) she will move to Florida if we can't get this done?"

I get it. If I didn't pick up more of the donation—sorry, investment— then I might really regret it in the future. I felt trapped.

"I will put in another $25,000."

All in: $35,000 for Olivia to stay with the coach she wants in a brand-new gym. They leased the building so all of the money raised was for the buildout and equipment. Let me be clear, the gym was magnificent: a big, open, huge space with high ceilings and state of the art equipment. It had a definite "wow" factor and had much more equipment as safety is always first and foremost, given the difficulty of learning a new skill. To give you an idea, they had a very cool foam pit, filled with lots and lots of pieces of foam, each about the size of a shoe box, for new, higher score–value tumbling moves. You could attempt a very difficult tumbling pass (that's what you call it when they diagonally cross the designated space for their floor routine) knowing you are going to safely land in the foam-filled pit until you are ready to try it on the actual floor and work on sticking your landing. They also had a great tumbling track, which is very bouncy, again for attempting new moves, and it will come into play in a later story.

Olga's gym is an immediate huge success. This clearly goes to Olga's head. In no time, she starts complaining. She needs more time with the girls, and lays a heavy-duty guilt trip on them when they might want to take a long weekend out of town with their parents, guilt when they have to leave early because they have tons of homework or a huge test the next day, and so on. These girls were in high school, and the workload was far more demanding than grammar and middle school. During Olga's time as a competitive gymnast, you are owned by the country. In her case, the Soviet Union. No one cared about your education. It was all about winning for your country. She had her way and had no desire to change her way. As Olivia has told you, both of them were stubborn.

Quick aside: Knowing you want to follow a collegiate gymnastics career does require you to keep your grades up in high school. University of Michigan is a very good, tough school. While her talent got her in, she was still required to achieve certain grades while in high school to qualify for the scholarship. You couldn't slack off.

I remember Olivia and I had a blowout back in April 2009 when my fourth book, *The 7-Day Energy Surge*, came out. Back then, my firm had a relationship with a hotel, and they agreed to throw me a launch party. I could invite a couple hundred people there on a Friday night from 7:00–9:00 p.m. Training went until 8:30 p.m., and Olivia told me she wasn't coming to my launch party because Olga wouldn't allow her practice to end early on that one occasion. I told Olivia that she could go from 4:00 until 6:00, then come home and get cleaned up and dressed for the party. When I heard that this was not well-received by Olga, I thought, *Tough shit!*

Now, as she becomes more and more of a "gym-zilla," Olga wants the girls to work on holidays, as in Thanksgiving, Christmas, New Year's Day, Memorial Day, Fourth of July—every holiday. Come on, she already gets them six days a week. I hear other parents of athletes complain about hard long weekly practice sessions, but no one I knew in *any* other sport was expected to train on major holidays. We are talking about the six major holidays here. That's six days. *Come on*, I thought. Most of the mothers are complaining and, being one of the only dads around more often, we ask for a meeting.

I am the designated voice of the group. Olga arrives, folds her hands, and tries to shoot me a steely snarl. I'm thinking, *Sorry honey, much smarter, far more powerful people have snarled at me in the past. I'm not intimidated by you or your attempt at a stare down.*

I called the meeting, so I begin:

"Olga, the parents and I have been talking, and we don't appreciate the guilt you put on our daughters and the fact that you now want them to train on holidays. We don't get very much time with them, between school and training, and we want to make it clear that we don't agree with holiday training. Also, we insist that you tone down the guilt when they have homework or tests and have to either miss or leave early from practice for important reasons. Many of them are stressed enough as it is, balancing school and their sport"

Olga employs the same snarl she tried on me, nostrils flaring and all. I just realized this is probably why she and Olivia got on so well. They both make that same face when pissed. In silence, Olga looks around the room, and each of the mothers, as if they have rehearsed, say, "Oh Olga, we never said that. We are fine with whatever you want."

I was thrown under the bus. Ellen was also at the meeting, and she agreed that the moms full on jointly threw me under the bus.

But wait, there's more.

A production company comes to Chicago to explore a reality TV show, tentatively entitled, "Mothers." I was going to be the token father. I have been asked a number of times to be a part of some type of reality show because I have some high-profile clients. The problem is the producers always assume my clients will be cool with being on camera, or even simply shown walking in and out of my studios. Not going to happen. However, this opportunity intrigued me because it was more about being a parent, and of course, I thought it could help my business and lead to future books, speeches, endorsements, and more clients.

I sit my kids down and explain something like this may or may not happen. They are probably eleven and fifteen, and they do look a little confused since their understanding of reality TV has been centered around watching the Kardashians. Don't get me started. I don't allow the kids to watch it when I'm around. Just the sound of Kim saying, "Ccclllloooooeeee" makes my skin crawl. I explain this show will be much different.

Olivia comes home from the gym the following Saturday and states she absolutely refuses to be included in any way in the show.

"Why such a strong opinion?"

"Olga told me not to do it. So, I refuse to participate in any way."

I called Olga and left a message and she called me back and I'll admit I was totally unhinged while on the phone with her. Bad words! Many bad words! Loud. Emotional. Clearly, this was not just about her intrusion in a family decision; this was ignited by years of seeing Olivia pressured to do things the way Olga wanted them to be done. Her way was not necessarily what was in Olivia's best interest. She behaved as if she had no respect for our time as a family. Only her needs mattered.

In retrospect, maybe not my best decision and especially not the best delivery.

I was summoned into a meeting with Olga, Roberta, who is now helping her run the successful gym and Ellen. Talk about tension . . .

Olga, folded hands, snarling nostrils.

Roberta, attempting to look authoritative and not like the "Desperate Housewife" she is.

"So, what are we here to talk about?" clearly knowing.

"How dare you speak to me the way you did on the phone?"

"You know why I was upset as I told you. I don't want you parenting our child. And this is especially hurtful after all I have done to make this place such a success."

Roberta, chimes in, "What have we ever asked of you?"

"Like $35,000, or Olga was going to move to Florida."

Here comes the big finish, after a long, uncomfortable silence from Olga:

"I wish you were never born."

A lot of people have said mean things behind my back or to my face, but this was a whole new level.

"Well, if I wasn't born, Olivia wouldn't be born."

More uncomfortable silence.

Then I realized, if I did not apologize, Olivia, her star, was going to possibly get tossed from the gym. It would be idiotic for both Olga and Roberta to do this, but I wasn't willing to take that risk. So, I proceeded to apologize for everything, over and over again. It was required but in no way heartfelt.

Absolute torture.

After that, we each kept a good distance from each other. I didn't want to do anything to jeopardize Olivia's gymnastics career since it truly defined her.

Parents, don't be surprised if you find yourself in a similar bind. Olga had the power and the upper hand. She knew it. She had it because of all the time she had with Olivia. It's hard to write, but in some respects,

Olga came before both Ellen and me. It's not uncommon, but it sucked. I'm not the only parent of an athlete who has experienced this type of behavior. As the parents, we have to decide what is best for our child. It may not always be what we believe is right or what is in our best interest.

Roberta immediately gave me my money back, plus interest. I assume (I'm not sure) she personally invested another $35,000 for the 10 percent interest. She intimately knew the financials of the gym and had assurances it would provide this rate of return and the ultimate payback of capital, which it did.

As Olivia was graduating from Latin and would be starting Michigan in the fall, the gym did throw a lovely farewell party for her. April, one of the moms, had experience in video editing. She created a truly terrific video of Olivia's club years, complete with still photos and actual video footage of her training and competing. It included pictures of Ellen and other family members. Was I in the video? I bet you know the answer.

Olivia invited Olga and her daughter to one of her last competitions at the Crisler Center at Michigan. She warned me, "Olga is coming because I want her to be there," and I said to her exactly what I said to Olga as she entered our row at the meet.

"You were there at the beginning. It only makes sense for you to be here at the end."

Olga and I hugged, then mutually snarled at each other. Done!

Readers, note: Olivia *way* toned down this section from my first draft. She insisted, and I caved in, something I rarely do. Can you even imagine what I originally wrote?

Chapter 7

THE BOOBS AND THE BACK

CONFESSION—*I hate my double D's.*

It was January of my freshman year when Olga opened her own gym. WGM, a local TV station in Chicago, wanted to do a segment. I woke up so excited as I got to miss the first part of school for the early morning taping. When I got to the gym, all my pals were in their favorite leotards, and you could tell everyone spent a little extra time in front of the mirror. I know I did.

To warm up our bodies, we stretched for the first thirty minutes, as we were told the camera crew would arrive around 6:45. This was my first time doing any form of live TV, so my heart was racing. I was both nervous and excited. Olga strategically placed everyone on different apparatus to make the gym look lively and busy. She wanted a lot of movement. She also wanted us to show off our best talents. I was thrilled to showcase floor, which you now know has always been my "happy place."

Truth, my back was not good at this point. I was frequently in pain. Sometimes my legs would even go numb. FYI, I never told my parents because my fear was they would keep me from practice and competing and insist on taking me to the doctor.

Olga personally went through this pain, as she had similar issues at this age. I did tell her my back hurt. I just didn't tell her the extent of the hurt.

Olga made the executive decision to allow me to tumble but on a softer surface with more give. AKA, the tumbling track my dad described earlier that was so cool and safe in the new gym. That's where you learn a new, oftentimes more difficult pass with more give and a softer landing. For this day, and the live performance, this was going to be my place to shine.

At 7:25 a.m., we are given the one-minute warning; we were going live, and I was the first to be showcased. 5–4–3–2–1, and the red light turned on the camera. I remember the female anchor began to interview Olga, which was my cue to take off. We planned that I was going to showcase one of the hardest skills on floor in gymnastics, a double layout. This movement is two flips backwards in a row, in the air, with your body completely laid out and long, as if on a board. It's a very pretty movement and requires precise hyperextension of your back. Height, power, and elegance were essential. Olga knew I had all three skills locked and loaded for the camera.

I remember taking my first step into my run for this pass and felt that familiar shock down my left leg. We did learn from a young age that, in gymnastics, when you are competing and performing, you go. I also didn't want to let Olga down, as I knew this was a big deal for the new gym and her reputation as a coach.

Normally, my body goes on autopilot. It just knows what I want it to do because I have practiced this move thousands of times. This was one of the few moments in my career where I had to think through every aspect

Confessions of a **DIVISION-I ATHLETE**

of this pass since I was very aware of how my body felt. Something was clearly wrong because it didn't feel good at all.

Once I had punched or hit the ground to take off for the double layout, I felt relief. The pounding in my back had stopped with the running once I was flipping in the air. I wasn't on my usual autopilot. I was very aware of the impending landing and potentially, the painful shot.

For a split second, while in the air, I thought, *This won't be so bad as I'm going to land on a softer surface.* Wrong. Pain. I wasn't prepared for this level of pain. I put my acting face on and made the landing look effortless. It wasn't. It hurt. It really hurt.

Once I saw the camera had turned, I got down and slowly crawled off the tumbling track, which is raised, onto the gym floor. Each slight movement caused the same shock of pain down my left leg. I tried to get up and walk and couldn't. The independent athlete in me wanted to coolly walk off the floor. The kid in me just wanted to cry and call my mom.

I continued to crawl on the floor behind the elevated tumbling track until a fellow teammate saw what I was doing. I saw the look on her face as if to say, "WTF?" She realized it had to be bad. My mom was picking both of us after the segment to drop her at her school and then me at mine. I knew at that point there was no way I was walking through the halls to math class in this pain. FYI, I wasn't doing well in math, so for just a split second, that eased some of the pain. Then it was back.

I called my mom to come pick us up earlier than we had planned. I also asked her to come into the gym, something I rarely did. As I've said, the gym is my place, my temple, and I didn't like some of the other moms who would come and watch practice, and of course, criticize. I only wanted my parents to watch me compete. That just felt right. Today was different. Something was wrong.

My teammate and my mom helped me out to the car. They both knew I would never ask for help had it not been serious. I couldn't sit up. Instead, I laid down in the backseat with my head on my teammate. The gym was located close to two major streets and intersections. Early on, we figured out a short cut to avoid them to save time. Unfortunately, this route included speed bumps, and when we hit the first one, I screamed. My mom immediately started driving a little faster. She knew we needed to go see someone ASAP.

We still dropped my teammate off at her school, and as she got out of the car, she said she was willing to help in any way. Mom drove directly to the nearest imaging lab where you can just walk in and get an x-ray, as there was no time to get it ordered the conventional way.

The doctor looked at the image for all of a moment and said, "Your L-5 is fractured."

I looked at him, puzzled.

"You have fractured your back."

My first question was "Can I compete in January?" and he laughed.

This was my first major injury, but not my last.

Chapter 8
YOUTUBE AND GOOGLE: FRIEND OR FOE?

CONFESSIONS—*I have an eating disorder.*

When I first started gymnastics, food wasn't an issue.

I looked forward to going home to eat after a hard practice. My favorite food in the world was buttered pasta with marinara sauce and real shredded Parmesan cheese on top, a roll, and a Trader Joe's sparking lemonade chaser. Carbs, carbs, and more carbs, and some sugar. I never once gained weight.

Granted, I was little, and I could eat whatever I wanted with the amount of activity I did six days a week. Any snack or any meal was in-bounds. As a kid, I never once counted calories. I actually didn't know what a calorie was. Was it fat? Was it a carb? What does it look like? Who comes up with it?

The only time my weight was ever addressed was when I was in second grade. I briefly had an additional coach, who worked with us while Olga's attention was given to the older girls. He was also Eastern European. He made his opinion very clear: weight and appearance were the key to success.

Plus, he weighed us every day. I actually don't know if Olga was aware of this or not, but before each practice, we had to step on the scale. If you look at the pictures included in this book, you will see one of me in the air, with my pigtails flying. Yep, that was my size at the time, yet he felt he needed to weigh us. Seriously sick.

Right around this time, Olga started inviting girls from the team to a three-hour acrobatic gymnastics practice on Saturdays. She did this type of gymnastics in the Soviet Union and wanted to bring it to the States. This is not the same as the usual gymnastics. This is partner, acrobatic gymnastics, or as we called it, "Acro." Olga wanted us to experience this movement for continued body awareness, teamwork, and trust. We were only invited once Olga knew we were mature enough to rely on a partner. "Acro" has two specific positions—bases and tops. Bases hold up their partner while the top performs the movement. Visualize the base standing with her arms up, holding the top performer in a handstand. Given my size, I was the top. In addition to this example, tops also struck other elegant and flexible poses. There were also times I would jump into my partner's arms. It was always done as a unit.

JIM INTERJECTION: Looking back, I find these moves were oddly hypersexualized. Most of the "bases" were girls, probably fourteen or fifteen years old, and were farther down the puberty path. Olivia was only seven. Way too much touching and contact. In retrospect, I'm disappointed in myself for allowing her to participate in these Saturday practices, but Olivia was living under a "Soviet spell" at the time.

"Dad, I disagree. It was team building, and I didn't think there was anything wrong with it."

"Well, you are wrong. Trust me; when you are a parent, you won't like it if you see it."

Confessions of a **DIVISION-I ATHLETE**

One Saturday I vividly remember, Olga couldn't be at practice at the old gym. Therefore, the male coach was the substitute. While this happened over fifteen years ago, I remember him commenting on the size of one of the girls who was a top.

"She should be a base, not a top," he said with his accented disdain, and insisted another girl take her place.

After that day, we never saw her again.

At virtually every practice, weight was brought up. I didn't understand why we were being lectured on weight instead of working on our skills. The other girls felt the same way. We hated him. I hated him. I quit.

This one coach made me briefly fall out of love with gymnastics, very early in my career. I signed up to learn movements, flips, and twists, and my goal was to challenge myself. It was my parents' goal to wear me out so I would calm down. Whatever our goal was, a weight lecture wasn't on my wish list.

Again, I quit.

For about two months, I didn't go to practice. First, I was relieved. Then I missed it. I've also been told I was once again a nut job at home. My mom talked to Olga and planned for me to come back for a practice and once again give it a try. When I walked in the gym, the male coach was only working with the boys. The girls were off the hook. I often wonder, if I had to be coached by him, would I have stayed? Probably not.

Outside of this one experience, weight and body image weren't central aspects of my gymnastics career.

Olga was unique. She came from a world where thin was in. That's the way it's done, and that's the expectation in the Soviet Union. Ironically, she never discussed unhealthy eating habits with us, which I now find extremely remarkable. Always the opposite. She made sure we ate, were fed on trips, and had energy to compete to the best of our ability. She never knew I struggled with weight issues.

I used to religiously watch YouTube videos of Russian Olympic legends as I identified with their skill and style. Gymnasts like Olga Korbut, Lilia Podkopaeva, Svetlana Khorkina, and Victoria Komova all weighed around 100 pounds yet competed brilliantly. I falsely believed their success came from the appearance of their body. I thought my success depended on my appearance in a leotard like them.

Then I went through puberty.

I got boobs, a butt, bigger thighs, and the aforementioned back problems. After six months of my back healing I was cleared to resume training. My weight depended on one thing and one thing only: could I flip on a beam, swing around a bar, compete a floor routine, and nail a vault? I didn't care what I looked like. I never needed the reassurance of a scale as I never weighed myself during my high school years in club. All that mattered to me was my ability to perform my routine, then stick my landing.

Side note: I don't think my back ever completely healed, as I still have pain to this day in the same spot. I will frequently find myself feeling sharp pain down my left leg and occasionally have to stand up from shooting pain after sitting for too long. Now that I think of it, my back hurt every day during gymnastics, I just had more severe pain that took precedence in my shoulder, Achilles, ankles, and wrists.

I will never forget the first time during my sophomore year I thought I was fat. I started Googling "How to Be Thin Quickly" and lo and behold, the definition of "bulimia" popped up. For the record, it is:

"An emotional disorder involving distortion of body image and an obsessive desire to lose weight. This has bouts of extreme over-eating followed by depression and self-induced vomiting, purging or fasting."

"Really?" you might think, "how did you not know what that was?" I was never around any other girls at high school except for a few because I was always at practice. No one shared this "strategy" with me. I now realize it's unfortunately not a solution but a sickness. My hands-on relationship with my fingers and my toilet lasted for around eight months until a health class at Latin addressed this topic and I learned the reality: this condition could be fatal.

Discussing this time in my life is not easy for me. In fact, both my mom and dad have asked me repeatedly, "Why didn't you tell us? Why didn't you ask for help?" I wish I knew. At the time, though, this was a *me* thing. This was something only I needed to experience and get through. Again, I have this desire to do everything myself. But, for the sake of easing my mental struggles with discussing this, let's refer to "bulimia" as my *good friend, Carl*. No need to keep writing the "B" word, which I still find difficult.

I knew I had to stop. I couldn't continue to put my body through this violent action. Nor could I look in the mirror and continue defining myself as the girl who had a *good friend, Carl*. I slowly reduced the frequency of *his* visits and started making better food choices. This took about four months. As much as I wish I could say right here that my *good friend, Carl* and I stopped hanging out every day and everything was completely okay, that is not the case. At the time, I never fully recovered from believing that my *good friend, Carl* was the quick acting answer to all of my appearance problems.

With time, I felt I partially overcame the dysmorphic view I had of myself.

Little did I know, my *good friend, Carl* and I were just "on a break!" Fellow *Friends* fans will understand this because every time Ross yells this on the show, it's with incredible passion for two reasons:

1. He loves Rachel. You know that. He knows that, but at certain times, the relationship was toxic and not working. That's me and *Carl*, as he helped me somewhat love my body, but this relationship was equally toxic.

2. Ross and Rachel never fully broke up. They merely were always just "on a break" until the last season when they ended up together. In my case, *Carl* and I are done. And, he was no friend!

> **JIM INTERJECTION:** As we finish writing I asked:
> "Are you and *Carl* really done? When was the last time you two got together?"
> "Dad, I can't even remember. It's been that long."

The point here is that no one ever told me to look a certain way (except for the jerky male coach when I was seven) or to eat or not eat certain things. This came from me. My goal was to be the best athlete I could be. If it meant I had to be thin, I was "all in." That is what drove me to the toxic relationship, and now breakup, with *Carl*.

Mind you, I have continued to have "issues." I just haven't gotten back with *Carl*, nor do I plan on ever getting back together again.

> **JIM INTERJECTION:** Once Olivia developed, she hated her boobs. During her sophomore year in high school, I vividly remember her crying as I drove her to practice and begging me, "Dad, can't we cut them down or cut them off?" I said, "When you are done competing and get a little older, I will happily find the right doctor, and we will go for a consultation and figure this out." I meant it. Most of my friends and clients who have had a breast reduction wish they had done it years earlier. The results are truly amazing as the scars have been vastly eliminated or strategically hidden. I'm sure Olivia will have the surgery sometime in her life, but this was not the time.

Chapter 9
BEAM DOWN

CONFESSION—*I'm the beam's bitch.*

For those of you who don't know the exact size of a balance beam, it's sixteen feet long, four inches wide, and four feet off the ground. On it, we are expected to flip, twist, perform, and land perfectly. You can't fall. You can't wobble. Your form needs to be exquisite from start to finish. Talk about nerve wracking. This event is often referred to as the one that "changes everything." It's either great or it destroys everything you've done before and after. I've done both—often.

Here's an ironic statement—I loved training beam but hated competing it. When I practiced it in club, I felt confident, fearless, and rock solid. It almost became fun—almost. I liked the challenge of perfection and accuracy each time I practiced. Plus, I loved the rush of doing a perfect beam routine and going for the dismount, knowing I could stick the landing. I craved the pressure it brought and the feeling I could get up there while making it look effortless for my coach, fellow teammates, and onlookers. In practice, I could do it.

Not in competition.

JIM INTERJECTION: Olivia and I just watched footage of the 2004 Women's All-Around Olympic Championships, and here is what we just heard from the commentators:

I used to lie in bed the night before a meet and think about how much I didn't want to get up there. My fearlessness and confidence completely disappeared when I thought about beam. No other apparatus gave me so much anxiety. In club competition before each apparatus, you have a designated warm-up period in which to get acclimated to the equipment. This is your chance to get a feel for the beam and your surroundings. Everyone says each beam is the same. Correction—people who don't do beam and have never been on a beam say that. All beams are different, and all competition environments are different. I had a system. I knew exactly what I was going to do to warm up. It never changed.

My dad tells me that before each speech, whether to a dozen people or 10,000, he mentally goes over the exact points he wants to address. Review bullet points, predetermine the order, have a beginning, middle, and end. If possible, get a feel for the space and the stage. Same prep routine. Follow the template and most of the time, successful speech.

I followed his lead with my beam warm-up. It's almost superstitious. Each week, my competition warm-up was a carbon copy of the warm-up from the prior week. During warm-up? I'm fine. Once it is over? Not fine as my rapidly beating heart starts. It felt like 200 beats per minute (my resting is around 55, to give perspective), and my legs would shake mercilessly. My hands and feet immediately started to sweat like crazy (not great on a beam), and my head was just not in it.

Time to compete.

In club competition I had a few teammates, but they were in different age groups. Therefore, I was lumped in with other teams. My order could not be determined. Order in a beam "lineup" is extremely important. But in these club competitions, since it was usually just me, it was randomly determined, and neither Olga nor I had a say since my "team" was composed of other competitors who were also solo or maybe in a pair.

Readers note: In college, your coach chooses your top six performers on each event, where only the top five scores will count since they drop the lowest one. So, being first is tough as the pressure is on you to set a tempered tone, as beam requires a lot of skill coupled with a calm temperament. Similarly, being last is hard because if there is a slip-up in the middle of the lineup, the pressure is all on her to hit a perfect routine in order to not have to count another mistake.

Let me help you understand how critical lineup is to beam. If the first person falls, there is a rather large probability this mistake will contaminate the beam with negative energy. The bitch wins when you fall. When you watch a fellow gymnast, whether teammate or competitor, nothing is more gut-wrenching than watching a fall. Same applies to ice skaters. We've all been there. It sucks. Sure, elite snow skiers fall, but then their run is over. Race car drivers crash, but generally, the crash results in their race ending for the day. But gymnastics is different. Why? Because you have to get back up there and finish. It's not like having a bad volley in tennis where you can come back and win the next point. Nope. You are required to finish a routine you already know has failed.

In my club days, I used to make a lot of nervous mistakes. This type of mistake usually comes from obsessing and being overly cautious, driven by the fear of messing up. I practiced very aggressively but held back during competition because of the pressure. Nervous mistakes also happen when you look—well, nervous. It's evident to you—to the crowd—to your parents—to your coach—to the other athletes and to the beam. I was the beam's bitch.

I tried not to show my fear, not to let my nerves take over. The fact remains, I hated being up there in a skimpy leotard. Lots of skin is exposed. You're essentially naked with no room to hide. You're on display on a four-inch-wide platform, four feet high. Everyone can see every inch of your body. You're being judged not only on your skills, but on how you look, your body, facial expressions—everything.

I've used a lot of imagery in my gymnastics career. I used to imagine the relief I knew I'd feel once I successfully dismounted the beam and was safely on the ground. In between mounting the beam and this feeling on the floor, I put my body in fast forward. You know when you fast forward through commercials while watching TV and everything is moving at a ridiculous speed? That was me on the beam. This phenomenon is what I later learned is called "rushy-itis."

When I was seven, my parents had a conference with my second grade teacher. I always tried to do well at school: raising my hand, asking questions, doing all of my homework, and taking it all seriously. Gymnastics conditioned me to want to thrive and succeed in every task I took on, and school was no different. During this meeting, my teacher made an interesting observation.

"Olivia is bright and always diligent with her work," she told my parents. "She just has some 'rushy-itis' during tests and makes careless mistakes."

It makes sense. When there were things I didn't enjoy doing, such as taking tests or getting on a beam to compete, I rushed to get done. It translated into my academics and my athletics without me knowing it. Now I do.

A few days after my parent meeting, my teacher asked me to stay a few minutes after school to talk. Of course, this immediately stressed me out because she was cutting into my limited time to get from school to practice. The good student in me wanted to make sure I showed my teacher I was serious about improving and willing to meet with her, but I was really antsy.

"Miss Olivia," she began, "You are a smart girl with a strong work ethic."

I smiled. I knew I worked hard, and it was nice to hear her acknowledge it.

"You tend to rush a lot when you take tests. Tell me, what is six times seven?"

"42!" I answered proudly.

"Then why did you put 36 on your math test?" She slid my test out of the top drawer of her desk and turned it over, showing me the red X next to the question I answered incorrectly.

I knew the answer. I just rushed through it because I didn't want to take it anymore. I was done. I looked at the paper and wondered why on earth I made such a lousy, simple mistake. "Ah ha!" There's a perfect example of my "rushy-itis." I finally realized the similarity; rushing on a math test was the same as rushing on a beam routine.

Here's even more honesty: sometimes when I competed beam in club gymnastics, I would black out. I hardly remembered any of it. Think about how dangerous a beam routine is in general, and now think about losing control from fear and nervousness. Flipping with no mental awareness? That sounds safe.

I did this frequently, yet I distinctly recall one time in particular.

I was competing at this weird, indoor multi-purpose facility in the middle of nowhere. The place had turf on the ground and tarps all over to cover the turf for the meet. Simply put, they just dropped the four events inside this gross "arena" and called it the regional championships. It was a big meet—the biggest of the year with the most at stake—and it looked like an intramural attempt at gymnastics. The arena had a weird vibe.

Lucky me, I started on floor (the worst order), which meant I would end on beam. It's always alphabetical order from where you started.

> If you start on BArs,
>> then go to BEam,
>>> then go FLoor and
>>>> finish on VAult.

The first event determines the next three. Starting on floor means you go to vault, then bars, and conclude on beam. In my personal and slightly professional opinion, this is the hardest rotation. Think about it. What if you know you are going to have a tough conversation with someone and had to wait until the end of the day to do it? The whole day is ruined as it preys on your mind. This is exactly what it is like to end on beam.

Back to this competition. I don't like to brag since we make fun of braggers, but my floor routine rocked that day. It just felt right. It was crisp, fun, energetic, and with the right emotion. It was the whole package. I never rushed on floor. I always listened to the music to ensure I was hitting each movement to each beat.

I then went to vault, which at the time I would consider my second-best event. I landed well and received a near perfect score, 9.925. My personal best was a 9.95, and I had to wait until my sophomore year at Michigan to achieve that.

On to bars. I have always struggled the most on bars. I found early on that my body was made for the tumbling and power apparatus instead of the precise and more graceful movements on bars. I did well, as well as I could at the time, and was relieved to be three quarters of the way done with the meet. Now—beam!

My beam warmup went well. Nailed everything and felt solid. I was ready.

The judge saluted me. Saluting means they raise their arm to signal for you to begin. You can take about ten seconds before starting, but once the judge salutes you, it's go time. I remember a shiver of nerves shoot down my body and into my feet, and the sweating began.

Then, blackness.

I literally do not remember a thing except landing my dismount, saluting the judge to show I have concluded my routine and walking off for the coach hug. Other than that, nothing.

Fun fact: In researching exact dates and locations of referenced competitions, I found some old beam routines online. I *do not* recall these routines at all. I'm watching one from 2010. I was thirteen. Right now, literally *no recollection* of the routine. But, this made me smile. You can see the relieved look on my face when I land my dismount and I'm done. On this specific day, Karas—1, Beam—0. This was a rare occurrence.

"Olivusa," Olga said, "How on earth did you save your front tuck like you did?"

I looked at her kind of puzzled. What did she mean?

I guess my front flip was way off center. Once I landed, my body knew to readjust itself and keep myself from falling. I didn't know I saved the fall.

A male coach from an opposing gym came up and high-fived me. "I'm going to show this to my girls at the gym to show them that is how you save yourself from a fall!" He owns a gym in Illinois and watched the entire routine. I smiled and thanked him, still not remembering any of it. I thought about asking him if the rest of the routine was okay but decided not to look like a loser.

The next Monday at practice, I watched the video of the routine. We frequently watched them, much like football players analyze the game when it's over. I saw what I did. After the front flip, I was aggressively wobbling and literally grabbed the beam to pull myself back to center. Deduction for grabbing the beam, but it wasn't as bad as a fall, and I feel the judges are actually kind when they see you save yourself from a fall.

I never told anyone, until now, about my blackouts. I had them a lot, but this time stuck with me. "Where was my confidence?" I felt it on the other events, but beam took it from me during my club years.

Chapter 10
PERKS AND DINKS

CONFESSION—*I was a nobody in high school.*

High schools have their own sports and teams. These may include football, basketball, soccer, track, swimming, tennis, field hockey, golf, and so on. Athletes who participate in school sports enjoy certain "perks." The opposite is true for nontraditional, nonschool sports such as fencing, dance, horseback riding, gymnastics, archery, and so on. For those who participate in a more nontraditional activity outside of your school, you may experience certain "dinks."

Perk #1: Saves time. You're already at school, so you don't need to drive anywhere for practice. Everything is right there. No need to daily rush out and head to a completely different facility.

Dink #1: Eats time you don't have. As if the stress of your sport isn't enough, add in darting out of school and rushing into a car, starving, only to fight traffic, and hopefully get there in enough time to take a few deep breaths. If you are late, you are usually penalized with extra conditioning, or at the very least, public admonishment. Sure, there are those days when traffic lights are all in sync with your need to get there, class lets out a couple minutes early, you eat your snack in the car, and are not in a crappy mood. But truthfully? Rare.

Perk #2: Easy exceptions. Play for your school and early dismissal for a game/match requires zero to no effort. You play for them. Your coach (often also a PE teacher) is happy to walk upstairs, tell your advisor or teacher you need to be let out early with no penalty, and you're easily off to the game or match.

Dink #2: Hard exceptions. For a sport not associated with your school, everything is hard. It makes sense because the school can't allow students to randomly miss class or not show up for expected participation in events. I get it. During my club years, I needed parental consent and letters stating I would, in fact be traveling for a meet. Sometimes I needed a second confirmation letter from Olga. As if competing wasn't enough, add the stress of potentially being penalized for missing school. There was no blanket understanding, and I had to deal with each individual request, never knowing what the reaction would be. Plus, I was asking for their permission to go when I had a firm obligation to show up. It was a lot to handle.

Perk #3: PE Credits. Sport for your school equals "bye-bye" PE. Need I say more?

Dink #3: No PE Credits. I had to take PE as participation in a non-school sport didn't excuse me from daily PE. Could I have used the extra hour the Latin athletes got for studying and homework? Sure. Instead, I was expected to engage in intramural kick ball or pathetic three-on-three basketball in a sweaty, slippery gym. What if I got injured? Olga would have levitated. I did not want to see that. In May of my junior year, I won the all-around AA national championship, which we will write about later. Senior year I was excused from gym, as they finally got it.

SIDEBAR: High schools, get it together. Public, private, parochial, whatever, take a moment to get to know your student athletes and if he or she is deeply entrenched in their sport. Look at your PE requirement and accept more than reasonable equivalents. Just be smart.

Which takes me to the final perk:

Confessions of a **DIVISION-I ATHLETE**

Perk #4: Status. Your peers know you are an athlete, cheer for you, commend you for your skill and talent, and appreciate the fact you represent their school. Watch any TV show or movie and you tell me, do the school's athletes get special status? Yes! If you frequently win? Wow! You have buckets of social capital.

Dink #4: No Status. You're a nobody because you are never there. I never attended any high school social events. When kids talk about drinking for the first time at a friend's party in high school, I just laughed to myself. I overdosed on inhaling chalk, spent my Friday evenings after nine in bed with an ice pack or at Max's house with Chloe and Janet (my three besties then and now) watching a movie, again with an ice pack, or was asleep by 9:30. No one knew me in a social way, and my school was very social.

My freshman year, people started asking me why there was "white stuff" on my hands or on my clothes. Get your head out of the gutter because they were referring to chalk but didn't have a clue as to why anyone would have it all over them. Sometimes, I would come to school from an early practice or have chalk stained into my skin from the religious use of it. When I replied by explaining I do gymnastics, I would always get hit back with the same question. "Cool! Can you do a flip?"

This question makes all gymnasts crazy. Ask any gymnast. We all agree. Do you ask a baseball player, "Can you hit?" or "Can you catch?" Do you ask a swimmer, "Do you like the water?" Ask a soccer player, "Like to run after a ball?" No.

Finally fed up with the question, I decided early on to do something about it.

Latin has an annual Halloween costume competition divided into different categories. The student council president leads an all-school assembly where he or she will name a category, such as "Funniest Costume" or "Best Celebrity." Then, anyone dressed up in that category came up on stage, explained their costume, and hoped to win. The last category was always "Most Creative." As freshmen, we sat at the top, at the back end of the assembly hall. Getting down to the stage was a hike, but I had had enough. I jogged up onto the stage and waited my turn to explain my costume. I wasn't in a costume. I had absolutely zero costume-esque clothing on. When the microphone came over to me, I leaned forward and announced, "I'm a street gymnast" and right there did a back flip. The auditorium gasped. Dressed in blue jeans, a black sweatshirt, and tall Hunter rainboots, my "costume" couldn't have been less "street gymnast-y." Mind you, no one really knew my name or anything about me. I quickly became known as the "chick" who did a "flip" at Halloween. FYI, I didn't win the contest!

Later that day, I was greeted with many "Wow, I didn't know you could do that!" Really? They were shocked—a gymnast—could do a flip. That is how unknown my sport was to my peer group, which still seems so odd to me, given that it is one of the most popular summer Olympic sports. I say this in the nicest way possible. They knew nothing.

A little more history:

I was able to go to my junior prom in a dress my father thought was hideous—and it was—because it fell on a weekend after competition season had ended, which is always late April or May, depending on how far you got until Nationals. Competition season starts in December, making for a couple weeks of "leeway" at practice. Because of this, I didn't get to go to my senior prom. I was in Iowa for the national championship. I actually had a dress, which this time my dad liked because we picked it out together in New York; a date who my dad did *not* like, but that's another story; and a flight booked that would get me home in time to make it, although late. I felt it was this "rite of passage" to go to my senior prom, but I was so exhausted from the pressure and physical demand of the competition, I choose to instead go back to the hotel and bus it back in the morning. I really didn't care that I missed it. This competition was far more important. Only my three besties knew that my passion and love for gymnastics meant I needed to be in Iowa.

A few days after prom, we were in another assembly before school. Our student council president asked the school if anyone had any final announcements or remarks before we parted ways for class. Max raised his hand, something he rarely did at these assemblies. Max was the captain of the water polo team and also swam at Latin, so my initial thought was he was making an announcement for one of his teams. I was wrong.

He stood up and angled himself in a way so the entire auditorium could see his face and hear him say, "I don't know if any of you noticed—you probably didn't—but Liv wasn't at prom on Saturday." He paused. "Yep, that's right. She wasn't there because she was doing something much more important. She won a national championship. She was named the best gymnast in the country on vault and third in the all-around."

People began looking at me, and I couldn't take my eyes off Max. "So, if any of you bump into her, it would be nice for you to congratulate her on her successes as a gymnast outside of Latin. Congrats, Liv. We are so proud of you."

Then he sat down.

Some people smiled my way. I sat there stunned. I was trying to process what just happened.

People began congratulating me on the win, following it with, "I had no idea you were that good!" This was the only time in my high school years I ever felt noticed at school. Ever. Thanks, Max. I've probably never told you how much that meant to me.

Did I get noticed after graduating? Oh yes, word spread. This really amped up after winning the Big Ten Championship and Big Ten Freshman of the Year at the end of my first year at Michigan. People who didn't know I existed were now going out of their way to comment, "like," and congratulate me on social media. I also have been told my competition pictures are up on many walls at Latin. Interesting.

I always knew that my sport came with many more dinks than perks when it came to a high school social life. I never really gave it a second thought. The biggest perk for me was that I fell in love with gymnastics at a very early age. The actual sport itself allowed me to feel like I was flying—like I could complete the unimaginable in a high-pressure situation. The sport itself isn't the only aspect of gymnastics I fell in love with. I adored the control I felt over my body and my movements. I loved the punctuality and drive that gymnastics needed from its athletes. I lived for the strength of being a woman in a sport where I got to defy gravity while also competing with grit and passion. Then, when I went to Michigan and experienced the true meaning of competing on a team for something bigger than myself, I actually fell even deeper in love. I lived for the rush I would feel before competing an event, more so now as I was doing it for my teammates and my school. To me, this outweighed any prom, homecoming, Friday night party, or sleepover in high school and, eventually, any Saturday night out in college. This was my choice.

Now, no one knew that but my close friends. They knew my love and passion for all things gymnastics as they frequently came to see me compete. They understood what I did and why I did it. In retrospect, I do realize there were many social things I missed out on, but to my surprise, my history as a gymnast is playing a huge part in my new, unexpected social life in New York; more on that in chapter 24. The "dink" during high school is now a big "perk" post college.

If you are an aspiring, serious athlete, be prepared for sacrifices. If you compete or play for a club outside of your school, you probably won't get much attention at your high school. Even if you do compete for your school, you still need to focus on your grades and balance the stress of school with the stress of your sport. Don't rely on your sport to be what my dad called my "Golden Ticket." What if you get injured? What if you don't get attention from the schools you aspired to play for and attend? Then you have to fall back on your grades. It's a balancing act.

Athletes, ask yourself these two questions:

1. Why did I start my particular sport in the first place?
2. Do I want to excel at my sport badly enough to make all the other sacrifices that will be needed to get what I want?

Then, go talk to your parents.

Confessions of a **DIVISION-I ATHLETE**

Chapter 11
I'M A MICHIGAN DAD!

CONFESSION—*I have never been a big "rah-rah" guy.*

It's really not a part of my character. As I previously wrote, certain parents would scream like crazy while their daughter competed. I always thought, *This is about Olivia, not about drawing attention to me.* Oh, just an aside, both of my kids always say to me, "Look, everything isn't always about you," and I agree. This was 100 percent about Olivia.

I also have to come clean and share another confession. In the business world, I'm a bit of a big personality. I'm expected to energize and motivate people to generally do something they don't want to do. Opinionated? Yep. Provocative? You bet, because it gets noticed. Controversial? Sure, bring it on. My goal was to get attention, which brought more business, sold more books, whatever. "Business Jim," drew focus, and it was my "purpose."

"Competition Jim?" Low profile. As I said, I would sit there, smile, and send positive energy and then let out a big roar when she finished. During the actual execution of each routine? Nothing. No sound. No cheer. The last thing a competitive gymnast needs while performing a routine is unnecessary distraction, especially from their parents. They know our voices. They know if it is going well or not. Stay quiet. After they are done, or in between events (as we were expected to do at Michigan) go bat-shit crazy and add to the energy and excitement in the arena. The girls love that and feed on it.

Since my freshman year at Penn in 1979, I have been reading the *Wall Street Journal*.

Forty-plus years fly by fast. I skim the cover each day, then save the body of the paper to read over the weekend. Knowing that these competitions were painfully long, I used the event to multitask. Read a section. Watch a gymnast. Read another section. Check out another gymnast. Remember, Olivia was generally the only member of her team during her club years, as all the other girls dropped out or barely practiced enough to complete. Most athletes in high school are pretty connected to their coach, unless there is a geographical move or an ugly coach-competitor breakup. So, Olivia remained solo. It usually was just Ellen, her parents, Aunt Amy, wild Baba, oftentimes in Healey rolling shoes (I had to almost put a leash on him), the *Journal*, and me.

For her first competition in Ann Arbor as a freshman on the team, I wear my uniform; blue jeans, white shirt, blue blazer. Simple. No need to think. I travel and give a lot of speeches. When I pack, it's "grab and go." I had *no* idea that this could ever be considered inappropriate attire. When you are a fan of any Michigan sport, you *must* wear abundant Michigan garb. Nobody told me. No memo. No email. Nothing.

For the men, shirts, hats, overalls, headbands, blinking things to hold, and signs, sometimes with the picture of your child's head on it, which I found a little creepy. Women? Oh boy, all of the same plus headpieces, boas, big decals on their face of the block "M," and necklaces and rings and more blinking things!

I knew some of the parents from the official visit held in September of her senior year of high school for the girls joining the team the following fall. The event started at Michigan's football stadium, AKA, "The Big House." We had amazing seats at the fifty-yard line, the equivalent of fifth row center at the theater (that's how Olivia explained it to me), and we got to walk out on the football field before the game started. They didn't announce the girls or anything. It's just considered a BFD to be allowed to walk onto the field before the start. The girls were there on their final visit, before signing the papers to officially become Wolverines. I had no idea why people made such a thing about it, but once again, I knew nothing.

For her first meet, Olivia got me a Michigan hat. Between us, I look like a combination of a degenerate and a criminal when I wear a hat. I decided to just hold onto it. All Michigan home meets were at the Crisler Center. Men's and women's basketball are played there as well, so this wasn't a stadium just for gymnastics. Sometimes men's gymnastics, wresting, and volleyball could book Crisler since the arena seats 10,000 people. Yet, the women's gymnastics team calls Crisler home as Bev fought for the girls to complete in a real arena instead of a smaller and less championship-like arena. The parents always sat in the exact same area for all four years. As I started down the stairs—these are great seats, right in the center of the arena and the first ten rows—I got some odd stares. Why? I didn't know at the time. Now I do. I clearly was not properly dressed or adorned in Michigan garb, expected by all, especially as a parent.

I was also not properly prepared for the collegiate competition attire at this first meet. Wow, Olivia and her peeps wore sleeveless leotards with a whole lot of sparkles. As Olivia revealed earlier, in college, you warm up on all four apparatus. These sparkly leos were just for warmups. After this is over, they changed into the official competition leo. These include sleeves, and frequently more sparkles and glitter. Add to that the "M" decal on their right cheek, a "Flip for Chip" tattoo (special story later on) on the base of each girl's neck, tight, painfully braided hair pulled back, and all of them were in a small or extra small leo. Translation—not much coverage.

And nonstop screaming. It's deafening. From the moment they march out to be introduced, tons of shouting from the spectators. The louder you are, the more love the team feels. The sheer volume and relentless drone of screaming drove me insane.

Competition starts, and the *Journal* goes up as Olivia was later in the lineup. When she would compete, *Journal* down. When finished, and seeing her score, back up.

After the competition was over, I hugged Olivia (who covered my blazer with glitter), congratulated her (Michigan won!), and headed back to Chicago, about a three-and-a-half to four-hour drive depending on the hard press of your right foot. My phone rings and I see the caller ID—Olivia.

"Hi honey. How happy are you with your first win?"

"I'm fine, but *Dad*," not said in a very happy tone, "You *cannot* read the paper while my team competes!"

"Why? I've been doing it for years."

"I am a part of a team. You have to watch *the team*."

"But I don't care about *the team*. I only care about you."

"*Dad*, that's not what being a part of *the team* is all about. All the girls commented you had the paper up most of the time."

"Olivia, once again, I'm there for you, not a bunch of girls I barely know." Nothing against these girls, as most of them were lovely and also talented, but I had reading to catch up on and this was my jam.

"You *have* to watch the whole team. No paper reading again."

She shut me down.

The *Journal* and I broke up while watching competitions. It was painful, but we both got over it.

Then I received my "Michigan Dad" t-shirt from Olivia in the mail a few days later from the "M" den. That's the name of the Michigan stores that are everywhere, both on and off the Michigan campus in Ann Arbor and in all the stadiums, constantly packed with enthusiastic buyers of everything U of M. It's not subtle. Nothing about Michigan is subtle.

I got it, no paper reading *and* must wear a Michigan shirt, and the same shirt for every competition as I began to get very superstitious about what I was wearing when Olivia and her team were winning—and they were winning a lot.

Chapter 12
SCORING

CONFESSION—*I never got a perfect 10.*

Scoring is the most subjective and difficult aspect of gymnastics to explain. We all love watching the flips and twists and fun routines, but many ask me questions like, "Why is one gymnast given a score compared to another?" Or, "Wait, didn't she wobble? Why did she get a high score?" Honestly, I don't think anyone understands scoring, even the judges.

Many will agree that figure skaters are subjected to similar judging subjectivity. We have that in common. My dad told me that in the olden days, tennis matches had a chair umpire who determined if a ball was in or not. They made the call. Some players had temper tantrums and arguments about whether the ball was in or not. Now a computer can overrule their call and do it immediately. I'm not sure how technology will take some of the subjectivity out of our scoring. I guess we will have to wait and see.

Embarrassing confession—recently, I have religiously watched old broadcasts of meets while dying on the Stairmaster. My keen understanding of scoring biases has grown by watching routines I thought were mediocre at best, yet scored nearly perfect.

There are rules for what judges should take a deduction for. I say "should" because sometimes they don't. Going back to my judging table on the Stairmaster, I'm shocked to see such obvious mistakes overlooked, either because they weren't paying attention or chose not to pay attention. Look, judges have opinions and favorites as well. That has worked for me and against me.

How Many Judges?

In regular competition season, there are two judges for each event, and the score is averaged. You did see the two individual scores each judge assigned, then they were averaged. When there are three to four teams for a larger meet, there are still only two judges per event. For conference championships meets and NCAA Regionals, there are four judges, and they drop the top and bottom score and take the average of the remaining two. For NCAA Championships, which Michigan made my sophomore and senior years, there are six judges and again, they drop the top and bottom and average the remaining four. We always liked when there were more judges because some, but not all, of the subjectivity could more likely be averaged out. However, if all of the judges are on the subjectivity train, then the scores can suck no matter how many judges there are.

Start Value

In collegiate gymnastics, your routine needs to consist of enough difficulty and "connections" to achieve a perfect 10 start value. Difficulty is obvious. Skills are awarded a certain level of difficulty according to numerous things. For instance, more twists and more flips mean more difficulty. Landing forwards instead of backwards is much harder, as you cannot see the ground. That is more difficult. Imagine, for instance, in figure skating. A single or double jump on the ice is not nearly as difficult as a triple axel. And a quadruple axel is harder because it contains more twists. You get the point.

A "connection" is the ability to perform two or more skills back to back, without hesitation, showing control and precision. No wobbling allowed in between the skills, or you will not earn the connection bonus. When watching collegiate gymnastics meet, you may see a judge place a card with a number such as 9.8 on their table after the gymnast salutes at the end of her routine. This indicates that the routine did not contain enough difficulty and connection bonus to achieve a 10-start value.

To be transparent, you could have a start value above 10 due to an increased amount of difficulty and connections. But the highest score you could ever receive would just be the 10, the perfect 10, so I'm not going to feel sorry for you if that's what you got or ever get.

Strategy

There are two opposing strategies for wowing the judges:

Strategy 1—Wow them with difficult elements done perfectly plus high-performance quality.

Strategy 2—Wow them with simple elements done perfectly plus high-performance quality.

Bev Plocki, my Michigan coach, firmly believed in strategy 1. Michigan never takes the easy way out. I had no interest in spending four years performing pretty basic routines. Snore. I always wanted to challenge myself and grow as an athlete.

This is also a big reason why Michigan was my first choice. I knew Bev's reputation with regard to strategy, and it aligned with mine. It also aligned with my four teams at Michigan. Keep in mind, every year, from my freshman to senior, was different as freshmen joined and then seniors graduate. We also had to deal with multiple injuries. But each team agreed, strategy 1 was important to all of us. We welcomed the challenge.

NOTE: We did sometimes lose meets to teams who embraced strategy 2. There were judges who clearly rewarded very simple routines done very well. Some competitors on a collegiate team may have done the same routine all four years. Again, bore.

SECOND NOTE: Elite is different. I remember a conversation during my sophomore year with my dad:

"I don't understand, how can a girl get at 16.5 score in the Olympics? That makes no sense."

"Dad, given the level of difficulty, a starting score is allowed to increase."

"Why?"

"In the Elite/Olympic world, the name of the game is do as many hard skills and connections as humanly possible. Then try to do it perfectly. But, if you mess up, normally it's okay because it's all about how much difficulty you can pack into a routine."

"Sounds like a huge difference. Would you have liked this option?"

"Hard no. Zero interest."

Dreaded Deductions

Let me get a little specific. Most deductions come in the form of a tenth of a point, 0.10. A step on any landing is generally a tenth off, so a possible 10 becomes a 9.9 if that was the only mistake or the judge didn't have a biased against the specific team. Then, there are half tenth deductions, 0.05. This would apply to a bent leg when it was supposed to be straight or a flexed rather than pointed toe.

You cannot take a quarter of a tenth deduction, but you can end up with a score with a quarter tenth. If one judge gives you a 9.9 and the other a 9.85, your score will be 9.875. Remember, they average the scores.

Again, for each event, six gymnasts compete, but only the top five scores are counted. You always drop the lowest score. To determine the all-around individual competitors, they simply add up your four individual scores if you compete in every event. It always starts out of 40, and actually one woman, Karin Lickey, of Georgia, scored a perfect 40. However, I've gone back and watched these routines and, "Honey, you were overscored." Same for the all-around winning team. The absolute top score would be 200, but every gymnast on the team would have to receive a perfect ten on each event. Hasn't happened to my knowledge. You simply add the top five scores from the four events and get the total.

How Close Is Close?

If you're having trouble grasping the concept of winning by a toe point, try understanding the concept of winning by a fingertip. Michael Phelps won the men's 100-meter butterfly by a one hundredth of a second. He edged out Serbia's Milorad Cavic, winning with a time of 50.58 seconds to Cavic's 50.59. Again, the only difference here is Phelps won because of technology. He literally hit the wall one hundredth of a second faster than Cavic. When we win by 0.025, it's because a judge judged us that much better than the opposing team. Same small margins, different means of receiving the time or score.

Here are a few of my personal experiences with scoring to give you more perspective:

1. My senior year in high school, I qualified to compete at the Nastia Liukin Cup—essentially the all-star meet for that season's level 10 (highest club level) gymnasts. You had to win another qualifying meet to get invited to the Nastia Cup, so it was a BFD when you got to go. The meet took place at the Dallas Cowboys arena, and Emma (my classmate at Michigan who you will learn more about later) and I actually competed there together.

   All in all, the meet went great, and the experience competing in that huge arena was a highlight of my career. I competed against many insanely talented gymnasts including Maddie Karr and Anna Glenn, who went on to compete at Denver and UCLA respectively. The final results:

- Maddie took first with a 38.275 all-around score.
- Anna took second with a 38.25 all-around score.
- I took third with a 38.225 all-around score.

Again, all of these scores were out of a possible 40.

Essentially, I got third because of a half tenth. The point of this story is to share the small margins of error that can subjectively differentiate first, second, and third-place positions.

2. My freshman year of college, we hosted the regional championships in Crisler Arena. As I will share in my "Beam Up" chapter, I fell on beam and started this meet off poorly. Then our beam champion also fell. We therefore had to count a fall in our beam rotation. That all but eliminates any chance to win.

But, at our final bar rotation, something truly incredible happened. It started with Nichelle, who got a 9.875. Then came Austin, 9.875.

Then Lindsay, who got a 9.95.

Then me, 9.95 (shocking!)

Then Brianna 9.95.

Then Nico 9.95

Four 9.95's in a row. The only time, ever, during my four years at Michigan.

JIM INTERJECTION: Bars was never Michigan's jam. Of course, they were competent, but bars were more of a "have to do" rather than a "love to do," and most of the girls agree.

Watching 9.95 after 9.95 after 9.95 after 9.95 was crazy exciting. They were in the zone. As much as a fall can contaminate a lineup, a great performance followed by another great performance can also be infectious. I was wildly screaming and cheering and sitting on the edge of my chair. As I've repeatedly mentioned, that's not my usual reaction. They were all near-perfect routines, only marketed down one-half of one tenth. Wow. Almost my most exciting meet as a "Michigan Dad." It was a huge comeback, and I was crazy proud of how Olivia and her team fought back, even if they missed going to Nationals that year by just 0.05, even with counting a fall.

3. One final scoring anecdote—This past year, my senior year, we once again hosted the regional championships at Crisler Arena. The meet was absolutely stacked with talent between Alabama, Nebraska, UCLA, and us all competing for the two coveted spots that qualify for Nationals. Your placement during the season doesn't matter. It is ultimately just this meet that determines who goes to Nationals and who stays home. And this was that meet during my senior and final year.

We ended on vault, which is a hard event to end on. It is hard because we had a solid, high-octane floor rotation and were feeding off the energy of the crowd. With vault, you need to be powerful and explosive, then rein it in for the necessary "stick." We had a solid performance, but no one stuck their landing, so deductions were taken. We had to sit and wait for Alabama to finish the meet on beam to determine which two teams were going to go. It felt close. UCLA had already finished and claimed their first position, so it was between the two of us to claim the second.

The last Alabama girl stuck her beam dismount after her near-perfect routine. Within seconds, the final tally of scores came up on the Jumbotron showing:

Alabama—197.225

Michigan—197.275

Michigan edged out Alabama by one-half of a tenth. We went ape-shit crazy, and so did the arena. This is actually my all-time favorite memory at Michigan and will go down in history as my favorite gymnastics meet ever.

NOTE: If you want to see this moment when we found out we qualified for Nationals, go on @UMichWGym on Twitter and find the video in their tweets. It is honestly the most hysterical video ever and a bonus feature of getting to see my ugly cry and how my teammates had to physically hold me up from sobbing.

JIM INTERJECTION: I was hoarse for days from all the screaming. All of the Michigan parents couldn't stop. Then there was some crying, and I'm proud of Steve McLean and Ken Osman for being my crying buddies in the stands. I'm talking three grown men hugging with projectile tears. It was so unbelievably exciting. Just so you understand, we were prepared for this to be the last time we ever watched our girls compete. With this win, not only did Olivia and her team get one more "hit," but so did we as the parents.

While this chapter is Olivia's, I do have one score story I will never forget. It's level 10 in Jackson, Mississippi, when Olivia was seventeen. This is a national meet, so a lot of people and a lot of commotion. Olivia is doing well, but at this point, I'm used to her doing well. This isn't bragging. It's simply a fact, and boy did she put in the time to earn it.

For this club meet, they actually have an Excel spreadsheet on a computer, and they are projecting the spreadsheet on a large screen. I assumed it was brought in for this event as it didn't come down from the ceiling or attach to the wall. It just had three tripod legs, similar to what we had in my childhood basement growing up to watch old family movies.

As the competition is coming to a close, a gentleman in questionable Bermuda shorts taps me on the shoulder and says:

"Your daughter is Olivia, right?

"Yes."

"Take a look at the girl in the purple on bars and the girl on beam in pink. If both of them score under 9.8, your daughter will be the all-around champion."

I was in shock. I lean over to Ellen and tell her what he said, and she is in shock. We get up, right in front of the screen, and wait for the final tally as right now, O Karas is firmly in the number three position. As we looked up, with our mouths open, we watched exactly what the man told me would happen. O Karas hit the top spot with an all-around score of 38.4, beating out the number two competitor, who got a 38.225.

JIM INTERJECTION (CONTINUED): WOW! Another moment. We see Olivia gathering her stuff as if nothing special is happening and then see Olga walk over and put her hands on Olivia's shoulders. We can't hear what Olga says, but Olivia hits the floor in shock, and starts crying. Now we are all crying, and it's a little reminiscent of the final montage in *Notting Hill* when Julia Roberts takes Hugh Grant to the Academy Awards, and they get out of the car. All the cameras point to us and interviewers with microphones rush toward not only Olivia and Olga, but Ellen and me as well. Wild. All because of 0.175 points.

Bev and Judging

A coach's job is to fight for their athletes and fight for their scores. As I wrote earlier in this chapter, each gymnast is required to do a certain number of challenging elements and connections. I struggled with managing my strengths and weaknesses. I was really powerful but struggled with flexibility. I could jump high but had to fight for a good split. My coaches and I worked as a team to create routines that highlighted my strengths and minimized my non-strengths. On my buddy, the beam, I did a back flip called a gainer. Most gymnasts who perform this move take off on one leg, do a back flip, then land on the other. Yet, for me, I needed to make an adjustment.

I rolled and hurt my right ankle a lot during my career. No surprise. I later tore my Achilles on the same side. Because of the right foot issue, we "tweaked" my gainer. I would take off on my left leg and switch my legs in the air, landing once again on the left foot. That move was my dad's favorite on the beam, even though we shared a mutual hatred for the beam not known to me at the time. For four years, I believed Bev's judging inquiry came from the judges missing this skill. It actually didn't.

I recently talked to Bev about my beam routine inquiries, and she shared with me that the confusion actually came from the jump combination I did. Much like the gainer and the hard-to-see airborne leg switch, the jump contained similar elements. I jumped, started to split with one leg, then quickly switched legs to present a perfect split position in the air. I then connected this skill to another jump to receive a bonus tenth. Many times, the judges missed this and rewarded me with a lower-valued skill. Bev was always ready with her inquiry form to explain the skill to them and fight for me and a higher score. I've given you many examples of teams winning by one-half of a tenth of a point. We needed her to fight for us.

My junior year, I completed a vault that possibly was my personal best. Height, amplitude, capped off with a stuck landing. My score? 9.875. One judge claims she saw my arm bend. Bev was on it and immediately protested. She showed the judge a video of the vault taken by one of Michigan's managers, and there was no bent arm to be seen. Did she change her score? With the video evidence? Nope. Why? I don't know. We will never know.

Commentators and Judging

JIM INTERJECTION: Since I watch a lot of meets when not there in person, sometimes even the commentators are shocked by the judging. But like the judges, they clearly have their favorites, and Olivia was very fortunate to be one of them.

Evan and I were visiting universities on the East Coast and traveling by train from New York City to Philadelphia to visit Penn. It was February of Olivia's junior year, and we were live streaming a home meet against the University of Maryland at Crisler. We were so happy the Wi-Fi was strong enough on this train for us to have a great connection. Olivia was the second-to-last competitor on floor. She was having a blowout floor routine, powerful, flawless, perfectly stuck landings and clearly a big grin with each land. Evan and I were also grinning, and both of us were leaning closer to my computer screen and kept saying, in unison, "*Wow*" after her first two tumbling passes (she always did a total of three) The Big Ten commentators, always incredibly gracious and supportive of her, were also going wild, as in excited, as they literally said, live, "This may be Olivia Karas's first perfect ten floor routine." I said to Evan, "This is it. It's finally *happening*." All that was left was the last tumbling pass, a pass she had performed hundreds if not thousands of times in the past. She soared in the air, looking like nothing was wrong, and had huge height. Then, suddenly she landed on her hands and knees, something I had never seen her do before. I've seen her fall and make some mistakes but have never seen her look so defeated on the ground.

Evan and I both gasped. The Big Ten commentators were all clearly also in shock, as it's very rare to see a gymnast stay down on the floor. From watching Olivia and her team, I have noticed the underlying grit and mental toughness that comes when the girls fall. They always hop right back up, no matter what, and keep going. This time was different. The commentators immediately said, "Something has to be terribly wrong as we have never seen Olivia Karas do something like this." They were right.

We sat watching my phone, waiting for the call. It was Ellen's phone, but it was Olivia:

"Dad, I tore my Achilles."

"Are you in pain, honey?"

"No, just shock."

Her junior year competition season was over.

I will always believe that floor routine was going to be Olivia's perfect 10.

Sell It

Okay, I explained the two strategies a team can employ to win at competition. There is also an unwritten third—just "sell it!"

My senior year, I was coming back from the dreaded Achilles tear Dad just shared and it was time for me to compete on the exact same floor where I went down eleven months prior. Talk about anxiety! I wasn't quite ready yet to perform the full difficulty of my junior year routine, as we did change both the music and the moves each year. So Bev and I utilized the second strategy of "simple elements done perfectly plus high-performance value," to get my confidence back on floor.

In the middle of my second tumbling pass, I awkwardly punched the floor, leading to an obvious mistake and clear deduction. I was supposed to do a laid-out flip and instead did an amateurish and ugly cannonball tuck. I smiled after the pass, acting as if I did nothing wrong. My student coach, Sam Roy, always stood in the corner of that second pass. Some of us really need that support during our floor routines. Scott Sherman, who coached floor, was always there in the corner after I landed my first tumbling pass, but that was more for safely in case I went flying when landing my opening double Arabian. I didn't need the support on my third since I knew I was done. Upon landing my mistake, she smiled and mouthed, "Keep going." I finished the routine acting as if I did nothing wrong. My score? 9.875, which should have been a 9.6 at best! I got the benefit of the doubt. Bev said to me after the meet, "Thank God you smiled after that pass. They clearly missed it."

Many of you may know the name Katelyn Ohashi. She graduated from UCLA in 2019 and is a new friend of mine through the gym world. We were working a camp called Beam Queen Bootcamp and began swapping judging stories. We were supposed to be coaching but were laughing hysterically at each other's honest tales of tricking the judges. Katelyn went super viral in 2019 with her perfect 10 floor routine and has become a household name on account of it. She was so "on" for that routine, selling it, having a blast to amazing music and with equally amazing moves.

I remember telling her my stories about routines I did that scored *huge* but were painfully bad. She and I were rolling on the ground laughing when she shared with me that her viral "perfect 10" actually missed a requirement and should have had a start value of a 9.8, meaning a perfect 10 was impossible. There should have been a deduction as she duplicated a portion of a tumbling pass from a previous tumbling pass, which clearly the judges didn't notice. But who cares when you stick your tumbling, moon walk to Michael Jackson and dance to Tina Turner? I'd give her a 10 just for music choice. Katelyn, thanks for allowing me to share.

Fellow athletes who get judged, remember you can do a God-awful routine, but smile and look like you're having fun to trick the judges into thinking the routine was fantastic. Fair? Probably not. True? Oh yes!

JIM INTERJECTION: To illustrate this issue of how certain stars and certain schools are scored, read on. I'm not allowed to mention the gymnast or the team, but at one home meet, the opposing team competed on bars. One of their stars did a handstand which didn't hit twelve o'clock, as in straight up; it was closer to ten o'clock and a clear deduction. The score? Perfect 10. I asked the parents right around me, "Did you see that second handstand?" and made a straight hand gesture at ten o'clock, and they all agreed. But yes, perfect 10. Oh boy, some really bad language came out of me. When I asked Olivia after the meet, she said without skipping a beat, "Oh, the judges frequently don't even watch her routines. They just give her a 10. She's just one of their favorites."

But hey, don't let this subjective scoring discourage you. I never received a perfect 10 in my career but know of at least three routines I did that were "10 worthy." As long as you know you did your best, who really cares?

Chapter 13
IS THIN STILL IN?

CONFESSION—*I started counting calories.*

By my freshman year of college, I had achieved a healthy relationship with food and how I looked. In March, before Big Tens (we won!), Bev literally pulled me aside to make sure I was eating. *Wow, someone is asking me if I'm eating?* I thought. What a rush. I never thought I looked "too" thin or unhealthy. It was reassuring to share with her that the dining hall and I got along very well.

During my final three years in college, food and weight were back on my mind. It all started after I had wrist surgery in August 2016, just prior to my sophomore year. My right wrist had been bothering me during the second half of my freshman season and was progressively getting worse. Structurally, my ulna bones in both arms were already longer. Then, as a result of the repeated pounding and pressure on my wrists, these bones started irritating my tendons, causing a pinching pain. Unfortunately for me, the situation caused not only pain but numbness in my right hand. I know of a few girls who have similarly enlarged ulnas, but I have never heard anyone report the numbness I experienced. Numbness in your hand while performing a giant on the high bar is a dangerous situation if you lose the ability to continue holding on.

I got a few cortisone shots, as many athletes, not just gymnasts, dabble with them as a solution to an issue. It's totally legal and can take more than one treatment to provide a solution. I had two. The shot was supposed to reduce pain and inflammation and I got them both in my right wrist. Unfortunately, no luck. Now we explored surgical options, and there were two:

Option 1—Scope into the wrist and see what's up. No real cutting.

Option 2—A far more extensive surgery, which would shave down my ulna bone in my right arm. FYI, I'm also right-handed so clearly this wrist took more of the abuse.

My mom, dad, Bev (appalled at the recovery time of the second option), family friend, Dr. Brian Cole (who took care of my ankles in Chicago), my athletic trainer, Lisa Haas, and my fabulous surgeon Dr. Jeffrey Lawton all decided a wrist scope was the best option.

After a successful surgery, I was feeling relieved we went with option one and actually struggled eating food because I had to do it with my left hand. Yet despite the difficulties lifting the fork, I still ate a very similar diet minus the twenty-plus hours each week of training.

I really didn't visually notice any change in my appearance. Sure, my jeans got tighter, but we lived in yoga pants, sweats, practice shorts, and a sports bra or a leo, which all gave me room to grow. How was I supposed to notice? When I was cleared to come back to the gym, I struggled. Why couldn't I do a bar routine without panting? Why was one tumbling pass so much more difficult than it used to be? Why did my dismounts jolt my body a little more than I remembered? Finally, for the first time in my life, I voluntarily stepped on the scale in the training room. I was 140 solid pounds, and I remember playing with the scale, the real, balance beam doctor's scale, which doesn't lie and you can't manipulate it. You know, the truth you experience at your annual physical when you are told you weigh eight more pounds than you thought. The scale balanced. It was true. I was the heaviest I've ever been.

The number haunted me. It reminded me daily of my failure to remain fit and active during my recovery. It led me to believe, because of the number, 140, my gymnastics ability was going down. I was destined to struggle. Now, weight became my focus for success. Let me be clear, weight is important in gymnastics. But so is knowing an athlete's muscle/fat ratio, which we measured quarterly with the Bod Pod. The Bod Pod is a high-tech body comp device. It looks like a big egg, and you get into it with compression shorts and a compression cap, something that looks like a bathing cap. It measures fat and lean muscle mass. The Pod and I were always friends, though I found the actual experience extremely claustrophobic.

> **JIM INTERJECTION:** Women have 12 percent essential body fat, meaning that this is the fat required for a woman's body to efficiently function. This fat is predominately attributable to breast and reproductive organs. Olivia's body fat percentage was always around 12 percent. She was good at this number, and I asked her a few times, "Do you ever miss a monthly period?" and she said, "No."
>
> When a woman's body fat goes below 12 percent, the periods stop because the body perceives there isn't enough food available to nourish a fetus to grow to full term. Therefore, the body shuts down the mechanism that could produce a pregnancy. This never happened to Olivia, and I trusted she would tell me if it did.

It's important to be fit and able to flail around equipment with as little cargo as possible. Cargo as in weight. Think of it this way:

Imagine climbing Mount Everest, a hard enough task. Now add a twenty-pound weighted vest—you know, because why not? Now walk up, but don't forget to do a flip every fifteen minutes and land perfectly on your feet. Doesn't everyone do that when they climb a mountain?

That is precisely what it's like to do a bar routine with additional cargo.

You mount the bar, hopefully not too tired. Then start swinging, feeling good. When you're carrying more cargo, your ability to swing to a handstand, the hallmark of a successful bar routine, is drastically more difficult. You hold the position for a moment, then you have to swing down. The extra weight helps propel you around the bar, then turns on you as it makes it more difficult to stop for another handstand. Imagine swinging between the uneven bars to perform a release, a mandatory requirement. This is when you see a gymnast let go of the bar and move from the high bar to the low bar or vice-versa. The multiple handstands, the difficulty of your releases, and then your dismount pretty much determine your score. Post wrist surgery, I felt like someone put that twenty-pound vest on my body to test my ability, but I couldn't just take it off. It sucked. I panicked. I wanted it gone.

Did I revisit my old friend, *Carl?* No, I tried to get my act together. I did some extra lifting and extra cardio to be in the best shape possible. At that point, it worked.

What I did to my body to prepare for a meet didn't only affect me anymore. I had to be a role model for my team, a team player, and a representative of all things Michigan. That isn't to say I didn't think about *Carl* again. I lived with a teammate and fellow athlete who both personally struggled with their own *Carl*. This makes it really hard to leave the gym and come home to a supposedly safe place that was infected by not one but two toxic *Carls*. It was brutal. But at the end of the day, I went back to the whole embodiment of a team. Seeing *Carl* again was the same thing as falling off of beam and not working hard in the gym the next week to avoid falling again. I saw *Carl* as a forest fire who would burn anyone around me if I let him back in.

I firmly believe in the saying, "You're only as strong as your weakest link." In fact, I have experienced this through teams who succeeded due to strength from every member and teams who have failed because they had girls who dragged in their personal issues, whether they were mental or physical. *Carl* would have made me a weak link. I was not going to bring my team down because of him. Sometimes it truly does take a village.

Chapter 14
THE ESSENTIALS

CONFESSION—*As an athlete, I was much more superstitious than I thought.*

There are certain products and necessities gymnasts universally need. Some of these products or contraptions change over time. Some stay the same. Some are obvious, and some may surprise you.

Here are some of my essentials:

"Poise"

JIM INTERJECTION: I was recently eating dinner at my dining room table with Olivia and a bunch of her gymnast friends in town. At one point, the discussion begins about "poise."

"Are you talking about poise, like elegance?"

"No," Olivia says with her confused, nostril flare look. Yep, same annoyed look she shot me with her backpack on when she was ready to leave, early, for school. "Poise," she says slowly.

"Okay, what are you talking about?" I say as I make a grand gesture with my free hand, to illustrate I think we are talking about presentational skills when competing.

> *"Dad,"* said the same abrupt way she did when shooting down my *Journal* reading, "Poise, so we don't pee when we land."
>
> "What?"
>
> Olivia goes on to explain. If she didn't wear Poise, she would know, her teammates would probably know, and the floor and the mats would definitely know.

There was a meet in Cancun, Mexico, and Emma vaulted after me in the warmup lineup. This was pre-Poise. I was introduced to them a little bit later.

During warmup, Emma kept returning to our starting point, post landing, and asked, "Why do the mats have spurts of water on them right where I am supposed to land? Is something leaking on them? Did you see and feel it?"

"No," I said. "I don't see or feel it."

By the third turn, Emma finally realized nothing was leaking—except me. I was peeing each time I was landing my vault. From then on, I never missed a practice or competition without the help of my BFF, "Poise." My mom used to watch them on Amazon Prime and send multiple cases to me whenever they went on sale.

My teammate of three years, Lauren Marinez, introduced me to "Poise." I started providing them to other "pee-ers" on my team. This may sound a little gross, but bear with me. When we tumble on floor or land our vault, the impact can sometimes be so drastic that we leak a little. Nothing absurd, just a little. The problem comes from repetitions. Sure, doing it once and peeing a little isn't an issue. Try doing it twenty times. Then, we have an issue.

In no time, many of us were always "Poised." Every time I left the locker room, properly prepared inside and out, Lisa Hass would look at me and ask, "Are you Poised?" Each time I replied, "Oh I'm Poised all right."

My senior year, we had a male student athletic trainer who worked with Lisa named Sam Reed. Upon overhearing my typical "Poise" exchange with Lisa, he asked, "What does that mean?" Lisa looked at him and said, "You don't want to know."

Later when he found out, he said he could never watch female gymnastics the same way ever again.

Note: Now there are commercials for "Poise" all over the TV. The word is clearly out. "Poise" is not only for gymnasts, but many women post-partum with pelvic floor issues or simply weak bladder control. Ladies, we are all in this together.

Second note: Upon finishing my gymnastics career, with the help of "Poise," I wrote a letter to the customer service team at the Kimberly Clark Corporation, the makers of "Poise" and profusely thanked them.

"Tough Skin"

Lisa always carried at least three bottles of Tough Skin to each competition. It is a primer used before we tape up our injuries. It's basically sticky spray, so the tape doesn't move when you are sweating, swinging, and swirling.

Note: "Tough Skin" used to have more than one purpose. In 2006, the movie "Stick It" was released and still to this day remains the gymnastics bible. One of the famous scenes is where the gymnasts are spraying tough skin on their butts to keep their leos down. After seeing this movie, gymnasts all over the country experimented with this practice.

But at Michigan, we realized:

Hiked Leo = Higher Score

Then the "Tough Skin" never saw the butt area again. There wasn't an "ah ha" moment when we came to this conclusion about the hiked leo. We started to question why other competitors were getting higher scores and finally realized it had to be the "hike." Look, this happens a lot, especially with some teams in college who will remain nameless. Sometimes we would look at the leo. Yep, there was the hike. Then yep, there was a higher score.

Tape

Once the "Tough Skin" is sprayed, it's tape time. Many athletes rely on tape to hold them together while competing or playing. We gymnasts were not complete without our tape because it literally held us together. I always had tape on my left shoulder, both ankles, and the occasional wrist. There are many different types of tape. Some are thicker, thinner, stretchier, stronger, or stickier.

A lot goes into taping a body part. For instance, I was prone to blisters on my heels. If I didn't have lace pads with lube or a jell disc placed on my heels before applying the tape, we would have to cut it all off and start over. Emma used to have her shoulders literally taped down for stability as they were prone to popping out of their sockets. Prior to a meet, she would go into the training room, pull her leo down, with just a sports bra on, and Lisa would strategically zig zag tape in order for Emma to be safe to compete. Lisa and the Michigan Athletic Medicine team is really knowledgeable on taping modalities to assist in chronic pain. For me, I used a lot of tape on my ankles to secure them because they were very unstable. A lot of times, the tape serves as a mental reminder of any strained or painful body part—as if pain enough isn't an adequate reminder—and sometimes serves as a means of confidence that your body has a little extra help.

Hot Tamales

In my senior year, I began a love affair with Hot Tamales. My teammate, Maggie O'Hara, unfortunately suffered an Achilles pop like mine on the exact same movement, the back, double pike during our tumbling pass. She spent the season riding around on her scooter cheering on everyone as loudly as possible. I did the same when I was scooting around my junior year, but Maggie had something special in her front basket—the coveted Hot Tamales.

As my dad said, my first "crack" addiction was to gymnastics. Now I added a second addiction—Hot Tamales. Hot Tamales are a red-hot cinnamon candy, sold everywhere. They are literally all sugar, probably really bad for your teeth, but insanely addicting.

Before each routine, I did my usual visualization, lathered myself up with chalk, reached into her bin, and popped four Tamales just as my teammate before me landed her dismount. I was next. The Tamales were fast acting, and I do give them some credit for the extra energy at the end of my senior year when I needed it the most. Maggie even knew to scoot over close to me and be my "dealer." Talk about taking one for the team and being there for your teammates. Thank you, Maggie O'Hara, and Just Born, the makers of the coveted Tamales.

Bracelets

I wore four very special bracelets, which have their own meaning:

- One from my mom has the inscription "Celebrate Life."
- One from my dad has the inscription "Breathe."
- One from Cancun, a dolphin bracelet, which another teammate, Lexi Funk, also has. Lexi truly allows me to be completely and utterly myself, and I so appreciate this fact. We both bought these at the airport two minutes before boarding when we had remaining Mexican pesos and needed to get rid of them. This bracelet will always remind me to just be "me."
- One I bought for both Emma and me, which has the inscription "Fearless."

The reason I wear all four of these together is to remind myself to:

- Celebrate every day,
- Take a deep breath,
- Be a fearless badass, and
- Move through life like a dolphin in a dolphin show—fun and easy. I think about Lexi and me leaping out of the water in tandem, a classic show favorite. I like to think the dolphins enjoy it too.

I'm really not into expensive jewelry. These bracelets probably cost a combined $23.99, and the leftover pesos, but they mean the world to me. I wanted them visibly near me as you can't wear bracelets in competition. I wanted their energy. Stuck in a backpack was not enough. They had power, and they needed to be out and visible, so I always gave Sam Roy, our student coach, the dolphin and fearless and Maile Hermelyn, our assistant coach, celebrate life and breathe to wear while I competed.

The High Sign

JIM INTERJECTION: Back when Olivia was a club level 5 gymnast, I drove her to a meet and told her about the high sign from *The Little Rascals*. The "high sign" is where you put the top of your wrist under your chin, palm facing down, and wave two to three times. It's fast, but powerful. I always babbled before a meet in an attempt to take her mind off of it. I don't know if it worked. You are going to have to ask her. For some reason, I did the "high sign" to her at the start of this club level 5 competition as she walked out for warmups, and she did it right back and wasn't shy about it.

Now, during the "dark" years when Olivia was around thirteen to fifteen, I referred to her as a "Mean Swizzle

Stick with Boobs." She was super mean, and again, only to me, not her mother or brother. I've since learned a bit about Olivia being mean to Olga. That made me smile.

During these "terrible teens," I received a very half-assed "high sign." To be frank, it was a very rude "high sign." Ouch! It did hurt my feelings. Finally, by her junior year, she was back to shooting me a full on, confident, loving "wave." It was my superstition. We had to exchange the "high sign" before each meet. I remember I was running late, really late, to a meet her sophomore year at Michigan's Crisler. I ran down the stairs to the parents' seats and stood up on the lowest stair as they were just about to start the competition. They were beginning on vault, and at the last minute, Olivia looked up, and we exchanged the sign. It meant so much to both of us. I wasn't worried about missing the meet. I was worried about the tradition and the associated superstition. We continued the high sign until her senior year Nationals, Saturday, April 20, her last meet and the natural end of her career as a gymnast. For now, we have put the sign away since it served its purpose.

Maybe I will give it to her before we walk down the aisle someday.

Cheerios

Eating Cheerios the night before a meet with Emma was a ritual I was very superstitious about. We considered Cheerios our power food. Each time we traveled, one class, either freshmen, sophomores, juniors, or seniors, was assigned to make trail mix for the road. The trail mix was always healthy when Emma made it, but when Lexi and I got our hands on it, it was pretty much overpowered with M&Ms and Cheez-Its with some craisins and Cheerios. But the trail mix always had Cheerios in it. Something about those little O's.

"I love you, Emma McLean!"

The one other superstition I had my senior year was screaming "I love you, Emma McLean" before she began her floor routine. Normally I was after Emma, so I used every last ounce of energy to scream this at the top of my lungs before I had to begin my energy conservation for my own routine. This became one of our things.

In fact, a gymnastics fan attended one of our meets at Crisler and tweeted the next day, "Did anyone hear someone scream 'I love you, Emma McLean' before Emma started her routine?"

I was shocked at the influx of replies where people said, "Oh, that's Liv. She does that every time Emma competes floor." It was so cool to realize fans remembered that.

To bring it full circle, my last gymnastics meet was at the semifinals of the national championship in April 2019. Emma couldn't compete because she broke her hand the day before we left for the meet, so she was in a sling on the sidelines cheering us all on. However, that didn't stop us from our traditional night before Cheerio eating session on the hotel bed.

I walked onto the floor to compete what would be my final floor routine, and seconds before the music began, I heard, "I love you, Olivia Karas" come from Emma behind me. I instantly smiled. What a cool way to end a floor career.

Chapter 15
BEAM UP

CONFESSION—*The beam is my bitch.*

Good News—I'm an official Michigan gymnast.

Not So Good News—I'm still a beam black-outer.

I knew I needed to work on my beam confidence. I just had no clue how to begin.

It's my first day of practice as a D-I athlete. Lucky me, I started on beam in our first rotation. The team is split up into three groups, so the coaches have more time focusing on each athlete at each event. I was in a group with a new friend of mine, Talia or Tal, who to this day is still one of my besties. We all considered her the queen of the beam. Any beam task, assignment, or routine she did, she absolutely nailed. She was calm up there. Needless to say, she was the beam role model, our "beam-spiration" and anchored our beam lineup for all four of her years at Michigan. Her scores were—well, wow!

SIDEBAR: Tal was truly an amazing gymnast, but once I landed at Michigan, she was no longer competing on bars. Here's the story I had to share.

Talia Chiarelli and Nicole Artz started as freshman in 2013. Like Emma and me, they were inseparable, trained together, lived together, ate together, and competed together. During their sophomore year, Tal was cutting an avocado for dinner when she sliced open her hand, bad. She called to Nico, who was upstairs curling her hair, to come take a look. Nico said:

"I can't right now. I'm curling my hair."

"Okay," said Tal while holding a blood-soaked towel over the wound, "Just come down when you can."

She finally came down, and they both determined she needed to go to the ER.

As a result of the depth of the cut, Tal's relationship with bars had to end. Bars, more than the other three apparatus, are all about holding on, and Bev agreed it was best to keep Tal super strong on the other three events and not risk reopening or reinjuring the hand on bars. Plus, if you ask Tal, she hated bars, and I guess bars hated her. OMG I just realized this—she was the bar's bitch!

In practice, beam assignments focus on consistency, endurance, and confidence. Yet, there are two very different types of direction:

Quantity—This is simple. Just do five complete beam routines to measure your general consistency on that day. After the five, you are done no matter what. Don't worry about how good they are. Just get five of your specific choreographed routines under your belt. In my head I would think, *Just get it done. Five times. Whatever.*

Quality—Much more challenging because the coach is going to rely heavily on precision and perfection. We would be asked to do three complete beam routines without falling or if your first routine scored very well (the coaches knew how to score us similar to the judges), you only had to do one more and could opt out of the third. This time, I would think, *Get it done right. Zone in. Focus.*

"Olivia!" my head coach shrieked (she has a habit of doing that, which we all tease her about). Right from the start, I was super intimidated by Bev and wanted to please her with my work. When she called my name, I immediately stopped what I was doing and looked her way.

"Do you see Tal over there?" She motioned to Tal, who was over on the beam farthest away from ours, working as efficiently and perfectly as always. Don't get her skill confused with my "rushy-itis." There was no rushing here—her endurance was stellar, and her skill and technique were off the charts. She used speed to her advantage. She got everything done well in no time. She was a true beam superwoman.

Fun fact: In collegiate gymnastics, each girl is allowed a specific song in the background when she competes beam. This was not allowed in club. These songs range from slow and sad country music (which I never understood) to upbeat, confident, "power women" songs. Tal's was "Fancy," by Iggy Azalia. Look up the song and listen to it. It's Tal, on the beam, personified.

My first two years, my song was One Republic's "Stop and Stare," and my last two years it was Whitney Houston's "I Wanna Dance with Somebody."

Back to Bev—"If you can work the way Tal does, you are going to be a fantastic beam worker."

This phrase resonated with me throughout my four years of college. "Work the way Tal works." Efficiency and quality equaled success.

I worked really hard my freshman year to keep up with Tal and practiced my positive self-talk. I was a newbie on the team. I had a lot to learn about collegiate gymnastics, but beam was its own mountain to climb. Almost every gymnast I know has one event she struggles with. Beam is probably the most common since there truly is *no* margin for error. But many girls have their own distaste for one or two of the other events. I actually know girls who love beam. To each their own. But that beam messed with my head, for years.

Collegiate gymnastics is very different than club gymnastics for many reasons, the biggest of which are:

- Perfection is key. You had to perform difficult skills but with perfect execution. If the hardest skill had flaws, your score suffered, and it was in your best interest to keep it simple and let perfection prevail until you were ready to complete this skill.
- Presentation is rewarded. As I previously wrote, if you mess up, smile and act as if nothing happened, and hope your cute smile distracts the judges from writing down your mistake.
- The biggest difference—You're part of *the team*. Whatever you do affects more than just you.

My beam work improved, finally. Each October, we have an intrasquad at our training home, the Donald R. Shepherd Gymnastics Facility. It was beautiful. I truly felt honored to spend four years practicing there. When we first saw it, my dad said it reminded him of some amazing modern structure in a James Bond movie. It was so impressive.

As a freshman, this would be my first intrasquad. I quickly learned these are dress rehearsals for the predetermined lineup order, as it may be the first time we compete in this order. It's a way for the coaches to see if they like the lineup as a whole and to make sure each athlete felt comfortable in her respective spot. This is essentially a mock meet where you practice the pressure of going one at a time in your gym. But no bright lights. No uncomfortable leotard, and no painfully braided hair. No spectators, outside of your parents and boosters, just you, your team, and your coaches. Upon completion of the intrasquad, the coaches and the team all felt very confident in our lineups. Rarely was it changed with the exception of a last-minute injury.

Prior to the intrasquad, I was put in the six-person competition lineup. Bev was always writing down potential lineups, planning where to strategically place each athlete for the next meet. She keeps numerous notepads around the gym to jot down a new idea or potential order. For beam, which she personally coached, Bev stood at what we referred to as the "beam block." These are stackable, sturdy mats, which she made into her standing desk.

Following countless strategic thoughts on the lineup, Bev motioned me over to the "beam block" to ask me my thoughts. Again, all lineups require strategy, but on beam it was especially a challenge. A lot of thought goes into it as putting one athlete before another could either be super smart and make the next girl look even better or hurt the following competitor.

The first spot, the "leadoff," is an important position on each apparatus and is usually filled by the athlete who coaches agree will always deliver. The best quality for a "leadoff" is that they are consistent. This athlete's job is to start the lineup off strong and set the expectation for each subsequent competitor. A fabulous "leadoff" will also impress the judges. Similarly, a shaky and nervous "leadoff" sets a shaky and nervous vibe.

I was a freshman who still didn't understand all the strategy of lineups. I was just trying to stay on the beam and stick my landing. I did know the last person to go, the anchor, which was Tal, had the potential to score the highest. FYI—I was fortunate to have the anchor position a number of times in my Michigan career, but never on beam!

I made my way over to the "beam block" to talk to Bev. She looked at me, then down at one of her notepads, then right back up at me.

"What are your thoughts on going first?" as she gave me a hopeful look.

At the time, going first sounded great. I thought to myself, *First means I could rip the Band-Aid off sooner and be done, no waiting around painfully for my turn.* This sounded wonderful.

"I don't mind it at all! I actually would really like it."

Her face lit right up. It wasn't until later that I learned that no one ever wanted to go first on beam. Not only was I naïve, I was dumb because this position came with a ton of pressure.

My entire freshman season, I had the privilege (or pain, still not sure) of being first in our beam lineup. I definitely had my fair share of slipups but only two falls. Hey, not so bad. I was a freshman put in a pretty crucial role. Mistakes were expected and completely normal, but I did get better and liked getting it over with by going first. I was getting over most of my beam issues, and the "leadoff" position did help.

April 2, 2016. The regional championships held in Ann Arbor.

Regionals work as a stepping-stone to the national championships. It is based on your team's seeding after the conclusion of the regular season. This was based on your cumulative score against all teams in the nation. Much like March Madness in basketball, teams get paired with other teams based on their season standings.

In Regionals, there were six teams and only four events. Therefore, this specific competition had "byes." Bye rotations are essentially your gymnastics halftime. During a "bye," your team goes back to the locker room to rest while the other teams compete. Maybe you fix your makeup, yank your hair up a little higher, dance around a little, whatever. Byes were placed after beam and after vault. Therefore, our rotation went:

Beam,
    Bye,
        Floor,
            Vault,
                Bye and finally,
                    Bars.

Remember when I said starting on floor and ending on beam is the worst rotation? Starting on beam is arguably the second worst rotation.

Lucky us, we were given the most nerve-wracking event to start on in the most nerve-wracking meet of the year.

Ugh!

I could never quite explain to someone how awful it was to start your meet (or end it) on beam. Then I unexpectedly found a comparison:

The Tequila Shot

Starting on beam is like taking a tequila shot. You know it's coming. You dread it, like really dread it. Yet once it's over, you are one happy camper ready to party!

Tequila shots have three milestone steps.

Step 1: The Salt

Lick the top of your hand and place a generous amount of salt on the allotted area. This step is crucial, as the salt numbs what is to come. In beam terms, the salt is the chalk we use on our hands and feet. I used to lather my body in chalk before I went up on beam, thinking it would help my flop sweats. Simply speaking, the salt and the chalk are things we think will make the shot/routine easier. Alas, they don't do much but do mentally calm us.

Step 2: The Shot

Clearly, the worst part of the entire process is the liquid burning down your throat. In beam terms, the shot is the actual routine. It starts the moment you touch the beam to mount. This agony, like the shot, is not fully completed until you feel the burn down your throat or the prep to dismount. Which brings me to the concluding step . . .

Step 3: The Lime

Many people swear by sucking on a lime sliver (or if you're me, a lime chunk) to cushion the blow of the shot. The lime calms the burn. In gymnastics terms, the lime is the dismount. A zesty feeling emerges when your dismount has been successfully landed. You stick it. The relief. The happiness. It's done.

Now that I've clarified how a beam routine in competition is similar to a tequila shot, let me hop back to the story.

As I mentioned before, in collegiate gymnastics, you warm everything up in the beginning of the meet. But for safety purposes, each athlete competing is allotted a thirty-second rewarm up which is called a "touch" warm up. The timer for the "touch" goes off, making me aware that the uncontrollable shaking of my legs is about to begin for the next three minutes as the six competitors each get thirty seconds. Then, since I am first, the judge raised their right hand, signaling my cue to begin. I raised my arms in acknowledgement to start.

As you now know, I frequently blacked out on beam (or was it the tequila?) until my feet hit the ground. Yet, something D-I gymnastics does beautifully is teach you how to compete. My awareness of what I was doing had shifted. Although I am forever grateful for learning how to compete, in this moment, I wish I had just blacked out.

There is a requirement on beam called "the series." The series is pretty much what it sounds like—two skills in direct connection (remember how important connections are to scoring), showing the athlete's ability to seamlessly connect skills. "The series" I performed my entire career is called a back-handspring layout, or as Olga always called it, a flip-flop layout. If I had to pick one skill to aggressively destroy and never perform again, it's this damn flip-flop layout.

JIM INTERJECTION: I couldn't stand watching Olivia on the beam. It made me physically ill, and I knew the challenge and the pressure it placed on her.

Confessions of a **DIVISION-I ATHLETE**

Olivia interjection: Try actually doing it.

JIM INTERJECTION: I did get up on the beam once, actually, with your mom. We were at the team's annual tailgate, and for some reason, I thought I should.

Olivia interjection: How did you like it up there? Feel judged?

JIM INTERJECTION: It was brutal. Petrifying. It's really skinny, like just as wide as my feet. I don't know how you possibly flipped, twirled, and jumped on it. Weren't you petrified?

Olivia interjection: No. None of the moves scared me at all. It was competing beam that scared me. I loved to compete on everything else, but not beam.

JIM INTERJECTION: If I can find a legal place to do it, I'm happy to host a beam burning party. In an open space, we are going to douse one with gasoline, light that baby on fire, and watch it burn.

Back to the meet.

I'm doing pretty well in this routine—very aware, pretty poised (not that "Poise.") Finally, "the series." The key to this movement is being square on the beam. Everything you do from start to finish must be as straight and perfectly parallel as possible. I stood up ready to begin "the series." I raised my straight arms and realized I was ridiculously crooked. We haven't mentioned yet that I hesitated. So we will just say, I hesitated, trying to maneuver my body to get back on top of the beam for a safe and low deduction landing. My efforts were there, but it was useless. I landed on the beam with just my two biggest toes on my left foot gripping on for dear life. Realizing I was in a bit of a sticky situation, I bent over and grabbed the beam, as I did when I saved my routine in club. Yes, deduction, but I hoped to stay on. Unfortunately, it was too late. After holding on for a good three seconds, a long time in beam land, I fell off—another deduction. I hopped right back up, finished the routine, and ran over to high five my teammates. First event. First up. Biggest meet of the year. And I went down.

JIM INTERJECTION: Olivia was starting on beam, so I'm tense. Of course, Olivia's anxiety with regard to beam comes first and foremost, but I can speak for both Ellen and me, pre *and* post-divorce. We would look at each other as we waited for her to salute to begin her beam routine with this "Please, God (and neither of us are religious), let her stay on" face. I knew she was going down. She hesitated for one split second on her prep for the flip-flop layout (yes, I call it the same incorrect name like Olga, but that's what we knew it as) when she raised her hands straight up over her head. It was brutal watching Olivia go down on the layout. First regional meet of her freshman year, first apparatus, first in the lineup. Ouch! Then, the team's beam

Confessions of a **DIVISION-I ATHLETE**

> specialist *also* falls off the same beam in the same lineup. Therefore, a fall had to be counted, which generally indicates your likelihood of winning is almost zero. Brutal. I will miss a lot about her gymnastics career and watching her compete. I will not miss anything about the beam.

As the confession of this chapter is "The beam is my bitch," I know you must be thinking, "But you're still the beam's bitch and nothing has changed?" An accurate observation. But hang on for just a little more history.

I was in post-traumatic beam mode after this meet. Who was I to ever again think I should put a Michigan leotard on and compete for my school? I was the first person on the first event, and I went down. But I began to realize something.

I loved performing. The art of performing is taking mistakes or nerves and turning them into allies. You exude almost too much confidence in order to trick your brain into thinking you're confident and not nervous, even when you want to shit your pants—or leotard. So, if I loved performing, why couldn't I perform on beam?

My senior year is the only time in my entire sixteen-year career when I felt a genuine superiority over the beam. A combination of things led to this:

- Maile Hermelyn, our new assistant coach who wore my "special" bracelets when competing, and
- Déjà vu to Regionals 2016.

Maile's whole motto was to sell it. If you feel off, smile and sell it. In a brief period of time, she instinctively knew me well enough to know I thrived at performing. She taught me to treat competing on beam like floor, something I never put together. Dance, smile, wink, sell it, and teach the beam who is in charge.

It was a great idea, but I still hadn't bought into it yet. And it showed. We had our first competition of my senior year in Cancun, Mexico. I was first up on beam, first meet of the year, and first event of the meet. The only time I competed first on beam my senior year was this very meet, and what happened?

You guessed it! Down I went on "the series."

Enough! I finally bought into Maile's advice. Dancing on the beam and having fun, you know, making the beam my bitch, could work. That and I was never, ever allowed to go first on beam again, because clearly it wasn't my happy place.

Finally, it was working as I danced, smiled, winked, sold it and enjoyed my beam routines. I never again fell on my GD series. After years and years, and countless sleepless nights, stress and falls, I had successfully made the beam *my* bitch. Why didn't I figure this out sooner?

So, what is the point?

Whether you are a gymnast, an athlete, or anyone trying to overcome something you thought you would always struggle with, you can make anything your bitch. You will figure it out. We all have our own "beam" to master. Whether it's a person, place, position, our own procrastination, or an inability to persevere, just think to yourself:

> Dance,
> > Smile,
> > > Wink,
> > > > Sell it, and
> > > > > Enjoy it!

A motto I now live by. Give it a test drive the next time you are stuck.

Chapter 16
THE SECOND "SECOND" MOTHER

CONFESSION—*I didn't get her in the beginning. Now she's my inspiration..*

"Ladies," said in her signature squeal, will always be how I remember Bev. She would say this numerous times during practice, in between putting her glasses on to read her phone then returning them to the top of her head when done. Bev has been the U of M gymnastics coach for thirty-one years, and she shows no sign of fatigue.

Bev is the definition of a "Tiger Mom" in all the right ways. As I wrote in the scoring section, Bev was "on it" when she thought we were underscored in any way. No fear. She was "on it" when she knew about any team or personal issues which were affecting our physical and mental state. I know she felt her job was to protect us in every conceivable way. She truly succeeded, and that's a whole lot of "emotional estrogen" to manage 24/7.

Here's another perfect example. It was the night before the same senior year Cancun meet (when I just described my fall a few pages ago) and the Hard Rock Cafe was the place to be. Athletes sat at one table, coaches and some parents at another. Coaches and parents got their food right away and were finished while our table, the athlete table, sat with nothing. Another thirty minutes goes by and still, "No food for you," said in the accent of the Soup Nazi from "Seinfeld." My dad made me write this as he was a huge fan of the show. This night, we had an "Angry Beverly" on the loose.

She demanded to speak to managers, servers, you name it to understand why our food wasn't coming out. Another thirty minutes goes by and Bev finally gets an answer. The excuse? They ran out of shrimp. Next thing, we hear, loudly, "The next food that comes out of that kitchen BETTER be my athletes'! And if not, I'm going in there to make it myself because my girls are starving!"

We got our food two minutes later. She took care of us and took control.

As I previously wrote, Bev and her reputation were a big reason I made Michigan my first choice. Was I afraid of her? Yes. As I wrote about my first day of practice my freshman year, I also deeply wanted to please her. Therefore, I had mixed emotions about Bev. Part of me believes our relationship struggled in the beginning because she coached beam, and you know how I felt about it. Come on, I devoted two chapters to it.

Beam = Bev

By association,

Bev = No Bueno

It's not fair but it's the truth.

Looking back on it, I don't think I fully understood Bev as an underclassman. Therefore, I choose the easy option, not to like her. I didn't get her process and the true demands of coaching a team through twenty-four Big Ten championships. We all know there will be more.

FYI—This is a record. Bev holds more Big Ten titles than any coach in any sport in Big Ten history. Big Ten shouldn't be capitalized according to spellcheck but I don't care. This is the way I wanted it written. Such a privilege to have had her as my coach.

Once I got the beam, I got Bev. I'm sure this sounds silly to read, but it's true. My senior year was special for many reasons, and this was one of them. This shift I felt for Bev was profound.

During my senior year, Bev had to navigate a delicate situation that involved:

A coach.
My housemate and teammate.
A car in a mall parking lot at 9:00 a.m.
Steamed-up windows.
Dual arrests.

My dad and I are not trying to be coy and have an inside story we aren't sharing with you. This was a very stressful, very difficult, unfortunate, ugly situation—and *very* public. TMZ picked it up. You decide if you want to know more of the details beyond what we have written. Giving it anymore "attention" was something we simply did not want to do. But, given that the title of this book has the word "confessions" in it, we couldn't gloss over the situation without mentioning it. It was bad. Just trust us.

She handled this mess between the school, her superiors, this teammate, and us skillfully and gracefully. But there was nothing graceful about the situation. She had to protect many of the players. Now I understand it. At the time, it was confusing. We didn't get it. Now I do. Enough on said topic. It simply had to be referenced because it highlighted her ability to take on adversity, in and out of our sport, and protect the team and us individually.

Bev, "thank you." Not an easy job. Not a job with a lot of accolades, outside of the most wins of any coach in any sport, ever, in the Big Ten.

Final important story about Bev. Senior Night is very special because it is the last home meet and possibly the last time seniors compete at Crisler. After the meet, we walk onto the floor with our parents. Special, individual videos of our Michigan career are shown. My picure with my mom, dad, and brother is included in the photo section, and, FYI, it's the home screen of my iPhone.

The junior girls and their parents host a dinner in the Crisler party room, celebrating the graduating class. It includes a roast or skit, or whatever the juniors have cooked up for us. This year, the game Jenga was used to ask questions that had to fall into one of the following categories:

- Answered only by the team
- Answered only by the coaches
- Answered only by my parents and Emma's parents
- Answered by anyone.

Of course, when the question was asked to my parents and Emma's "Why did you first place your daughter in gymnastics," my dad blurts out, "Because she was driving us fu%&ing crazy." After a pause, the place went up.

> **JIM INTERJECTION:** That was a L O N G pause. I thought I made a terrible mistake.

> *Olivia interjection:* No, Dad, we loved it. And it was true.

When Bev was asked the final question, "What are you going to miss most about Olivia and Emma?" she froze. Bev doesn't freeze. It was a solid thirty seconds of silence and her looking down trying to gather her thoughts, before she said, "I just can't right now." Both Emma and I were shocked. Emma leaned over to me and asked, "What was that about?"

Our parents were equally astonished and confused because following the dinner, they said, "We are all surprised since Bev is never at a loss for words."

Bev later texted Emma and me and wrote, "I'm sorry I got choked up and couldn't articulate what I will miss about the two of you. You two represent everything I take pride in in our program."

Bev represents all the emotions, from shrill squawk to sensitive soul. I really did a total 180 in my understanding and love for Bev. Following our triumph in making it to the national championships, as I mentioned before, I remember hugging her as tightly as possible, something we started doing a lot my senior year following all of the celebration. The hug lasted about thirty seconds while we were still uncontrollably crying with excitement. Then I said something I never thought I would. As I hugged her tighter, I said, "I love you. Thank you." She gripped me a little tighter and replied, "I love you too, so much."

Chapter 17
INSIDER TRAINING

CONFESSION—*I didn't know I was an "insider" until I became an outsider.*

Insider Trading

Given his love of investing and *The Wall Street Journal*, my dad always talked about the stock market. He is very funny. Every time he wanted us to pay attention when he was going to make a point, he would raise his right index finger and proclaim, "Teaching opportunity." He wanted Evan and me to understand the stock market. So when I was obsessed with my first American Girl doll, Dad showed me in the *Journal* that American Girl was owned by the company Mattel, a publicly traded stock. He explained how the value of the stock went up and down with the company's performance, in addition to other factors. When Evan got his travel bug, which you will soon learn about, Dad would show him the stock of the airline we flew on (United) or the publicly traded hotel group we stayed at. He wanted us to understand business and, along the way, explained insider trading. That's illegal. That's where an investor profits on nonpublic information from an insider, most likely an employee of the company or someone with deep knowledge of the company, such as an attorney or investment advisor. Then he or she buys or sells the stock, or an option, and makes a profit. And possibly goes to jail.

As I have shared so much about my head coaches, Olga and Bev, I kept thinking, *but what about my "insider training?"* I experienced a lot of unique people and their unique approach to getting the most out of me, which isn't public knowledge. So here it is. Thankfully, no jail for sharing.

"Uncle" Dave Kuzara

Back in his day, Dave was a gymnast at Western Michigan. Since then, he has on and off been an assistant coach at U of M. I didn't know at the time, but it was Dave who pushed Bev to offer me a spot on the team.

Dave enthusiastically coached vault and floor, with humor. That's why he's "Uncle" Dave. Emma and I both loved floor. Vault. Yeah, no! At least not for me. But I know for sure that Emma and I shared floor as our personal favorite. You could see it when we competed.

My freshman year, when Emma and I spent the majority of our vault landings on our ass, he was always right there leaping up and chanting, "That was the best vault you have ever done!" As most gymnasts are perfectionists, I used to think, *No, Dave, it was not the best vault I have ever done.*

I know him well though. He must have thought, "Make them laugh. Make them enjoy it. Make them stick."

It worked. Our "stock" went up.

Our sophomore year, Emma went on to be the Big Ten vault champion and I was an All-American on vault at NCAA Nationals.

Lisa Hass

For over thirty years, Lisa has been the Michigan gymnastics trainer, and I firmly believe she is a "good" witch. Lisa says it like it is, with no apology or filter. "It" could be how to execute a move, how to repair an injury or imbalance, how to get out of a toxic relationship or away from a hormonal, emotional teammate (at the time), or how to just shut up and calm down. Keen intuition is what makes her a "good" witch.

My formula for gymnastics:

Athletic Ability +
Joy of Performing +
Strong Competitive
Spirit = SUCCESS

Top. Olivia had the focus (and the salute) from the beginning.
Once she set her mind to do something…"It's Happening!"

Bottom. I loved competing from the very beginning—at age 7.

Confessions of a Division-I Athlete

At age 13, I changed my signature look from pigtails to a ponytail.

Left. My nemesis—the beam.

Right. Wearing our all-silver leotards. Bev loves this leo, but we all thought it made us look like flying Frigidaires. This look eventually inspired our mantra: "You can't break steel."

Dad and daughter.

Top. I *loved* being part of the Michigan team. While individual scores count, it is the team score that matters, and everyone works together to win.

Bottom. My dad taught me to *persevere*. The beam taught me that if you fall off, you can get right back up and keep going. You have to compete on the beam if you are going to be an all-around competitor. I eventually made the beam *my* bitch.

Confessions of a Division-I Athlete

Top. Our family—Baba, Ellen (Mom), Olivia, and Jim (Dad). Competitive gymnastics is a family sport during the years of training, travel, competitions, tears, and cheers. It takes everyone to make it happen.

Bottom Left. My favorite photo of Evan and Oliva.

Bottom Right. I am a proud member of the "Michigan Dads"!

A proud Michigan graduate. Now what?

Confessions of a Division-I Athlete

We spent an enormous amount of time together after my Achilles pop my junior year and throughout my senior year. We met at the brand new 280,000 square foot Stephen M. Ross Athletic Campus. The construction cost was a modest $168 million. As I've said, Michigan alumni *love* their athletic teams and show the love, generously.

Lisa is notoriously known for coming up with nicknames:

Mine—"Liverlips" and don't ask me why, probably because I went by "Liv" at Latin and at Michigan, which my dad hated.

> **JIM INTERJECTION:** Who and what is this, Liv? You started it in high school, and I don't know why. People are calling you this name, and I don't know who they are talking about. Your name is Olivia.

Emma was "Em-cat."

Lexi—"Lexicon."

Abby Heiskell—"High School Musical." This was because her last name is pronounced "Hi-Scal," and if you say it fast enough, it becomes high school. Her name ultimately evolved to just "Musical."

Maddy Osman—"The Mad Dog."

Another new freshman named Maddie—"Mad Puppy."

Reema, who you will learn about later—"Wolver-Reema." It is still her Instagram name to this day.

One of the freshman classes (I'm going to leave out dates to protect the guilty, innocent, whatever) she actually named the "FSS"—The "Freshman Shit Show." In light of any obstacle, Lisa found a way to make us laugh.

She kept things light, which many times seemed impossible. For example, after a bad meet, she was showing my family the new Ross facility. In the state-of-the-art crew training area, my dad asked, "What happened at the meet last night?"

No pause: "It was a shit show."

"What happened to X, who had a rough meet?"

Again, no pause: "She shit the bed."

Final Fun Fact—Lisa is also ordained and has legally married numerous alumni. To be honest, I don't know the reason why she initially became ordained, but many people have asked her to marry them. In fact, it is already on my mind for when I get to that point.

What has Lisa taught me? Her favorite expression, "Keep it loose, keep it tight. Enjoy the journey and do your rehab exercises."

Lew Porchiazzo

My final insider was my strength and conditioning coach Lew Porchiazzo. Many Michigan athletes, not just gymnasts, who worked directly with him attribute much of their success to his role and guidance in the weight room. It sounds cheesy, but he really did piece us back together to make us the best possible versions of ourselves.

Just to be clear, Lisa was my athletic trainer who specifically worked with the injury. We met in the athletic training room to see her. Lew worked with me in the weight room where we worked on strengthening my entire body, not just the injured area, to both accelerate recovery and keep me strong and sane. Yes, both of them as a team instinctively knew I go crazy without some form of movement. The moment I was off crutches from the Achilles pop and surgery, I was in a boot and began partial weightbearing. Lew and Lisa devised a plan to put my other foot in a specific weight-lifting shoe to even me out (the boot is elevated, so brilliant solution) and taught me to do assisted bodyweight squats with a TRX. I thought, *Finally, I'm getting back to my pre-injury routine.*

However, Lew's true "insider" insight stems from far beyond weights and strength. He used to give the most badass motivational speeches to us, usually involving superb placement of expletives. Sometimes it was to kick us into gear, sometimes it was to compliment our work, and sometimes, it was just to remind us how lucky we *all* are to be Michigan Wolverines.

Lew and I also got along swimmingly as he and I both share an "insider" obsession with all things Dunkin'—the best coffee ever—and don't try to fight with us.

Here is the final example of what made Lew so special and essential to building us up, both mentally and physically. There was a *FloGymnastics* article about me titled, "Michigan Gymnast Olivia Karas' Comeback Is Complete." Lew immediately sent me a text that read, "Cool interview and piece. Big time proud of you, but hate the title. This (poop emoji) is far from complete. You are just getting better and better. Keep it up." Then his text ended with, "Go get a Dunkin' coffee to celebrate"

I want to make a final point about both Lisa and Lew. My Achilles tear was physical, sure, but the hardest work was mentally getting back to practice and competing post the "pop." I had to trust both of them when they would say, "You've got this. You're ready," because I didn't feel ready. I felt it could happen again, but this time, on the left side since I relied on it so much. Injured athletes, you have to know what I'm talking about. Overcoming the fear is hands-down the hardest part of coming back from a serious injury.

Why have I shared this insider *train*ing? I have because it is something you should have on your radar.

Athletes, and not just gymnasts, you should consider these points:

1. Whether you are looking to train and compete at school, in a club, or at a university or college, don't only fixate on the head coach. Try to get the know the other coaches and trainers because you may actually find they have more influence on you during your time with the team.

2. Go to university hosted camps during high school. It is a great way to get some face time with everyone. Go. Go to a lot if you may be

interested in more than one school or team. Don't just settle for the first one because this is a big decision.

3. Talk to the current team members. Don't just interact with one of them; talk to as many as possible since you may find many conflicting opinions.

4. Look at the other athletes at a camp or recruiting event. Do you see a common personality type? Would you want to spend four years with them?

Parents:

1. Observe how all the coaches interact with the competitors or players, not just the head coach, when you are watching a team your child may be interested in joining. I don't care if this is in person or on a live stream or on television. Keep your eyes open.

2. If possible, ask other parents about their son's or daughter's experience with all the coaches and trainers on this team. People ask my parents all the time about my experience and all my coaches and trainers at both the club and collegiate level. Some also asked why I didn't look at a specific school or team.

3. If you have the opportunity, ask the other members of the team specific questions. Don't just say, "How do you like it here?" Ask, "Who decides who plays or competes? Do you think it's fair? How do they help your when you are injured or behind in school?"

Then athletes and parents, sit down and compare notes. This is a big decision. Get a good feel for all the players. Get the "insider" information.

Chapter 18
BABA
Evan's Chapter

CONFESSION—*I was irrelevant.*

At Olivia's meets, I was either propagating the concession stands, desecrating a bathroom, Heely-ing around (those were my gym shoes with wheels, popular at the time—I know, lame), or screaming my face off while watching her compete. From a young age, I loved gymnastics. It's awesome to watch no matter how much or how little you know about the sport. However, I especially loved watching Olivia. First off, she was better than everybody else (what my dad wrote about her performance ability was right, as she was amazing) and could execute each and every move that much better. The most important thing was that she loved it. I could tell. I'm her brother. I remember a moment when she was at a level 7 competition. Her floor music stopped mid-routine, and the judges gave her the rare opportunity to restart her routine. All eyes were on Olivia, and as her creepy Russian spy music came on, she paraded her eighty-pound, fourth-grade figure around the floor. I know Olivia well enough to know that in those moments, she was actually having a great time rather than showing some teeth for an extra tenth. FYI, I wrote this chapter before knowing that Olivia recounted this exact same meet and situation with the music. It's funny what sticks in our minds, isn't it?

She was happy, so I was happy. Right? Wrong. Not how it works.

While these moments were amazing, the day-to-day was tough. My life was Olivia's life. I couldn't hang out with people after school because Olivia had to get to practice. I ate dinner at 9 p.m. because that's when she got home. Everything was scheduled around her. We arose at 7 a.m., which I didn't want to do because I like to sleep, and left school at 3:30 sharp. Then, I was either driven with her to the gym then home or was dropped off at home to perform my 4 p.m. duties (pun intended). *Everything* was scheduled around Olivia, and I hated it so much. I like to take my time. I like to chill. My nickname is "Baba" because as a little boy, I've been told I sat in my bouncy chair and was very "chill," unlike Olivia, more like a "Buddha," which my dad called me. When Olivia couldn't pronounce "Buddha," she called me "Ba." From there, I've been told as I was only a baby, my dad nicknamed me "Baba."

I don't like all this rushing shit, and Olivia and Jimothy (my dad hates this nickname) are the queen and king of losing their minds when I don't move fast enough.

I also couldn't go anywhere. From a young age, I've loved the hotel industry, and I've wanted to see the world. That's why I'm at the Cornell School of Hotel Administration. It continues to be my passion. Every day, I would go into my dad's room with a cool hotel or destination on the desktop and say, "Dad can we go here pleeeeeeeease." I always got the same answer, "Evan, we can't. Olivia has practice" or "Olivia has a meet." I felt trapped. I couldn't go. Olivia got to do what she loves, and I wasn't able to. Cool.

Over time, I bottled up my feelings of being scheduled and caged in until I rebelled. I refused to clean my room, refused to get out of bed, and refused to move quickly, especially when forced to. It also escalated my desire to travel. I wanted to jump off of stuff and climb mountains. As a part of a "structured" gymnastics family, who would listen to me when I wanted to say, "Hey, I'm here too. I don't like order. I crave disorder."

I manifested my wants for change and chaos in an obsession with Dubai, the epicenter of experiential insanity. I began my research in fourth grade. I picked out my dream hotel, Raffles Dubai, and my dream experiences, seeing the Dubai mall, watching the dancing fountains, riding the roller coaster at Ferrari World, and whipping down the waterslides at Atlantis. Then, I started begging. Once a week, I would go into my dad's room showing him another cool thing I discovered about Dubai. He either gave me the Olivia schtick or told me he couldn't because of work. I think he just wanted to switch it up so I didn't hold it against Olivia.

Three years later, we're sitting at Balena, a fantastic Italian restaurant that tragically burned down. It was my thirteenth birthday. When gifts rolled around, my dad handed me two envelopes. I was shocked. Our dad never gets us gifts for birthdays and Christmas because, as he puts it, "You get gifts all the time." Not today and not tonight. I got something special. I opened the first envelope and in it was my passport. Odd. Then the second envelope had a letter. As I opened the letter, I saw an itinerary for six days, five nights in Dubai, UAE. I started bawling. I don't cry often, but I was mouth crying in the middle of a nice Italian restaurant. And it went on and on. Audible sobbing.

Reflecting back on that experience, I cried so hard because it had been a while since I felt like my parents noticed me. Olivia's gymnastics took their attention, which makes sense. She was a star, and I, just like them, was so proud to be related to a star and allowed to exist under her "glow." But with that came a feeling that I was on the backburner. Sure, there were moments where I felt more appreciated. Whenever Olivia would invite me to sit with her during awards, whenever she would give me a trophy my mom had ordered called the "best brother" award, I felt relevant. It sounds pretty spoiled saying, "I needed a trip or a trophy or attention to feel like I was loved," but that's how it worked for me, I guess. I felt in that moment at the table that somebody had finally listened to me about what I wanted. I felt like someone cared.

There was a portion of my life where I felt like nobody cared about me. From my seventh grade to the end of my eighth, I hit my worst depression spiral to date. Every day, I was psychologically tormented at school because my "friends" would either treat me like a pet or throw me into lockers. One time, we were playing football, and somebody tackled me. I tried standing up. They started to kick. And kick. And kick. School sucked.

I would go home and cry. This was during the same period my family was going through a very difficult time collectively. I felt like everyone took their emotional baggage out on me. If somebody had a shitty day, they'd find something to yell at me about. At least that's how it felt. Home sucked too.

I developed the mentality that I was worthless. That literally nobody wanted me to be on this Earth. I used to have a recurring dream where I'd be walking a pirate ship plank, and I'd look back and see every person I had ever met screaming, "JUMP." I hated myself. I sucked.

I used to not be able to look in mirrors. I vividly remember one night when I was just thirteen. I had just gotten out of the shower and looked at my body in the mirror. I started to sob. My thoughts were violent—"Your ribs are showing. Hopefully somebody breaks every single one and puts you out of your misery," "Who could ever possibly respect you when you look like that?" "No wonder your parents don't pay attention to you as much as Olivia." That night was the first night I ever wanted to kill myself. I went out onto my balcony, looked down, and told myself, "Just try to make it through one more day." I cried myself to sleep. That was the first of many nights when I felt suicidal.

Before Dad and Olivia asked me to be included in their book and be a part of this chapter, I've never told my family that their constant attention towards Olivia threw gasoline on my already-present feelings of inadequacy. Being the sibling of a star isn't easy. There was a tweet going around from Madison Kocian's mom that I vividly remember seeing. It had a photo of Kocian and her little brother with the words, "On this day one year ago, my daughter became an Olympic gold medalist, and my son started his junior year!" I saw this look in his eyes that I recognized because I had seen it when I looked in the mirror. All I wanted to do was hug the kid and tell him, "Just try to make it through one more day." Being "the sibling" sucked.

I still have those feelings of inadequacy sometimes, especially when doing my sport, track and field. Contrary to what most people know, I am a D-I decathlete/heptathlete. I'm not very good. I'm no Olivia. I never will be Olivia at a sport. That feeling sucks. When you've grown up around an Olympic-potential sibling until she decided not to pursue this path, nothing you do will ever be good enough to take the spotlight away from your sibling. I've read this manuscript and have heard my dad say, "We never treated the kids unequally or picked favorites." That's bullshit. I don't care if your kid has a big brain (that's what he calls me) or is a big athlete, your kids are more than whatever box you put them in (yes this is directed at my father as it remains a point of disagreement). When you neglect, we notice.

But feelings of inadequacy aren't always bad. I channeled my fears into my personality. I became more energetic. More absurd. Significantly funnier. More social. More personable. Anything that would make people notice me and realize my worth, I did. It's gotten to the point where people tell me I bring unparalleled energy to the room and call me the life of the party because I'm getting people riled up on the dance floor. One time, at a track and field party, I was hanging onto the banister of our house's porch leaning over the crowd mouthing the words to "Pursuit of Happiness." After a lot of personal reflection, I've realized that my years of insane behavior stem from feeling neglected as a kid. I embrace that reality. My energy does *not* suck.

I credit these character developments to boarding school. My dad forced me to go, but it was the best thing that *ever* and *will ever* happen to me (Good work, Dad. Thank you). It gave me a place where I wasn't just "the sibling." I was Evan. I was my own person ready to attack the world. It took me until halfway through my junior year and an *unparalleled* support system of friends who I call my family, to realize my worth. But I got there, and that's what matters.

Being a part of Olivia's career has given me many gifts—my thirst to see the world, personal growth, and identity development. It has also been a mental parasite stripping me of any feelings that I'm good at stuff. *However*, if I were to put the gifts and parasites into a blender, add some almond milk, protein powder, and MCT oil, and blend that shit up into a signature Jim Karas shake, it would taste a hell of a lot more like a gift. For that, I say "thank you."

How's that for a confession?

Olivia's confession: I had no idea.

Hearing this from my baby brother is difficult, hard to read, and leaves me speechless. I had to read through it twice to fully let his words sink into my mind. I guess I was naïve to think it wasn't *this* bad.

As Evan mentioned above, he exudes energy and fun. From a very young age, he also exuded energy toward me at meets. I remember looking into the stands before I would compete and see him, with his long bushy hair, on the edge of the bleachers ready to watch me. His mouth full of braces, he always smiled at me and cheered each time I began and finished a routine.

Now that I look back, it must have been rough. Clearly it was.

Regardless of Evan's feelings he just shared, I only felt love. Every meet, every win, every loss, every day, he loved me unconditionally. That in itself speaks volumes to his character.

But Evan isn't just some sibling on the sidelines. He is an impressive track and field athlete. The one thing in this piece I will disagree with is his description of how he is as an athlete. He is honestly really good. He started a little later, so he is just now growing into his strides and getting comfortable with his own style of running and competing.

As I read and reread his piece, I took the time to sit by myself in my apartment and actively put myself in his position. I can honestly tell you that I have no idea how he did it. The unintentional neglect he wrote about, the "come along for the ride" feelings he must've felt, and the struggle with garnering my dad's, mom's and my attention had to have been brutal. He should have hated me.

If you are a sibling of a high-level athlete, read Evan's chapter. Understand his words. Believe his honesty. Is that you?

If you are the athlete competing at a high level (me), recognize how your sibling(s) must feel. Maybe talk to your parents about how to make them feel noticed, feel equally important. A "Best Brother" award and sitting with you at the awards ceremony is not enough. Make sacrifices like they do for you, every day. Don't be like me and look back now thinking, *Whoa, I really didn't make any sacrifices for him—ever.*

JIM'S CONFESSION: I completely missed it.

Evan's words and honesty have played over and over again in my mind. It's painful to read, painful to absorb, and painful to feel I "missed" something that should have been obvious at the time. I was ignored as a second child to my older brother. Growing up Greek, only the first male child rates. He receives all the attention. I can't completely relate to what Baba experienced with Olivia and her sport but can relate to being invisible a good deal of the time because of an older sibling. I would never have wanted this reality for him and should have been far more aware of what could be going through his young and then maturing head. I made a mistake. Okay, a big mistake.

Suicide? That was also a shock, a horrific shock, when I think of what could have happened. I actually have to move on from that thought.

To refresh your memory, back on page 31, I wrote, "Looking back, no one minded. No one complained. She was moving. She loved training. She was happy."

I should edit that line, but it's what I thought at the time, and our goal has been to be authentic and honest.

I assumed it was tough for him, but like Olivia just wrote, I really didn't know it was *this* bad.

I saw the hat with the propeller. Of course, it was a "look at me" choice. I remember when I bought you the Heelys with the wheels so you could sit back when you wanted to pick up some speed and zoom around. You mostly wore them at Olivia's meets. Again, I knew they were meant to draw some attention to you, but I didn't know, past the propeller and the wheels, when you were just hitting your teens, that it was this bad.

In my defense, and the whole family's defense, you never, ever said anything. I don't know if it's about being a boy, or a part of your character, but you should have said something to someone. You had a lot of people around you, both immediate and extended family, and friends who you could have talked to. I'm not going to go back, but in the future, Baba, talk to us. Parents with any child in the spotlight, make time to talk to the siblings. Don't just ask, "How are you?" Make it specific. Ask, "Are you okay with all the focus on your sibling?" Frequently ask because this is not a "one-and-done" question. Ask a lot.

I'm going to first go back to the Dubai trip since Baba highlighted it. Yes, I did start to realize the desire for something that was "his," and not "hers," was real. He just kept asking, over and over again, about a trip, but I have to come clean. I've been a 1K (which means you flew 100,000+ miles the previous year) on United for ages. That status comes with a lot of perks. I needed an additional 15,000 miles in 2013 to keep my 1K status in 2014. There were two options:

- Buy the 15,000 miles for around $5,000 or
- Fly the 15,000 miles.

I was fooling around in early November, trying to figure out how I could keep my status. I went to United.com, then reservations, and typed in Chicago to Dubai. OMG, it was just over 15,000 for the round trip. Some might call this divine intervention but since I'm not religious, I'll just go with a way to accomplish two things at once. My business class ticket was right around $5,000, and I could use miles for him to fly right next to me. Realizing this could be a solution to not one, but two issues, I texted Ellen and asked, "Can I take Baba to Dubai when holiday break starts and get him back for Christmas Eve?" She loved the idea, so I booked it.

Watching him open up the two envelopes at Balena and balling, I mean truly uncontrollable sobs, made *me* cry, again. We have it on video on my phone. He couldn't stop crying. I finally realized just how important this was. With a little external push from my ridiculous need to maintain my 1K status, it was a trip of a lifetime and definitely a turning point in our relationship. Travel then became our jam, and each year, we take another trip outside of the States, just the two of us. He does all the research and planning as he is "Mr. Travel" and has gone so far to produce complete, detailed itineraries.

The bullying? I didn't know about that. I'm not using this as an excuse, but I really didn't do much for decades but work, work, and more work. Since Evan was born until now, I have been running two businesses, writing six, soon to be seven, books, speaking sometimes all over the world, popping on TV every now and then, and for over a decade when the kids were growing up, commuting to New York almost every week. I wasn't an absentee parent, as I was around and made it a point to be around when I had the kids. I would instead call me a frequently "distracted" parent.

Is this an appropriate excuse for missing what was going on with Evan? "Hell no," which is another one of his favorite expressions, so I felt it was important to use it here. I should have seen your pain. I should have given more thought to the questions, "How is he doing through all of this? Does he hate Olivia? Does he hate me for providing what little time I have for the kids to making it all about Olivia?"

Fast forward to fall 2014. I made the executive decision: Evan was going to explore boarding school. This was by no means a desire to send him away. This was what I thought would be a great opportunity to get from under the "Olivia" spotlight, be his own person, and experience a whole new, unknown to him, "launch pad." I could have been corny and said I wanted him to "vault" into a new opportunity but will leave the gymnastics references to his sister.

He wanted nothing to do with it. I made him take the same tests Olivia had to take to get into high school. We visited boarding schools on two separate occasions. He was not happy. He got into Latin, the same high school Olivia went to, but no way was I letting him go there. He also got into Walter Peyton, an amazing magnet school in Chicago. A "magnet" is a special public school you have to test into. Given my zip code, he had to achieve a perfect entrance score on his exam. He "did it." Yes, he has a big brain and yes, when I say that, it pisses him off.

Latin—In.

Walter Payton—In.

So only the boarding schools' acceptances were left. I desperately wanted him to go to one as I knew it was the right place for him. I log onto the website on a specific day to find out if he got in. Here is how it went:

- Deerfield Academy—waitlisted—Bad language came out in my studio.
- St. Paul's—waitlisted—Worse language, close to my Olga rant, but this was to my computer, not a person.
- Choate—I was so annoyed, assuming another dink, I quickly skimmed the page.

I read, "Given your accomplishments . . ."

I think, "That's nice."

I read, "Given the volume of applications," and think, "Oh no. Not again,"

Then I go back up to the top and neglected to read the first two words—"You're in!"

Master Karas was not happy. I told him Latin was off the table. He had to choose Walter Peyton, two blocks from my home and *free* or Choate.

He told me he hated my guts. I told him I was almost forty years older and had forty more years of hate, so he wasn't going to win a hate match.

I know my kids are crazy close. I'm proud of this fact. Every Sunday, they would pack their bags and move from their mom's place, right next door to mine. In 2010, both Ellen and I moved to new apartments, but we were still very close in the city. But they did it together. They had each other. One of my greatest accomplishments, and I know Ellen agrees, is that our kids are *so* close. Being the child of divorced parents isn't fun. I know from my own experience. Evan relied a great deal on his sister and her support, and I worried about him in Chicago, alone once Olivia would leave for Michigan. Solo. Sister-less. But this is only one of the reasons I got so amped up about boarding school.

As I just wrote, I also instinctively knew Baba needed a different launch pad. Staying in Chicago would not provide such an experience, and I also had more evidence.

When I arrived at Penn, I had *no* idea what I was getting myself into. I didn't understand how it works on the East Coast let alone at an Ivy League school. I was clueless. I kept meeting men and women who had gone to boarding school. I thought only "bad" kids were sent away, something out of a Dicken's novel. I was wrong. Those who attended these schools totally had a leg up. They had their shit together. They knew how to manage time. They seemed more worldly, as they met kids from all over the country, even all over the world at their school, which is not the case at Latin where it's a bunch of rich kids who live in a few square miles. The kids I met at Penn were ahead—they had already spent one to four years on their own. It was a plus, not a minus.

He went. First two weeks? Bad. After a rough start, the best, as he wrote. Now he is blowing it out at Cornell. His goal is to someday own a luxury adventure chain of hotels, currently called the "K" hotels. If anyone can do it, he can.

Baba, sorry for the neglect. Sorry for the awful thoughts you had about, you know, the balcony. I can't say anything more than that.

I have been on television, on and off, since my first book was published back in 2001. Every now and then, I get recognized and sometimes approached. The kids just roll their eyes when someone says, "Are you Jim Karas?" as they know, the minute the person walks away, I will say something obnoxious like, "See, your father *is* a celebrity." They both tilt their heads and in unison, I get the condescending "Aaawww." Then, once Olivia was on TV for Michigan and winning, the camera would frequently cut up to Ellen and me applauding in the stands. Now, when I am in line to board a plane or at Starbucks, people will tap me and say, "Aren't you Olivia from Michigan's dad?" Only one word can describe how it makes me feel—love!

During parents' weekend at Choate, Baba's senior year, I have never had so many kids come up to me and say, "You must be Evan's dad." See, Evan literally looks like a "mini-me," so people immediately put us together. Each student said something like, "We love Evan. He's the best. He has been such a huge help to me this year." It was all praise, praise, praise. That was in October of his senior year.

In November of that same year, I went to recruiting event for prospective Choate students. We all wear name tags with the year our son or daughter graduated or was going to graduate. I walk in, get my glass of wine, and am chatting with a few prospective parents. From across the room, I hear, "Are you Evan's dad?" and a man and his son come rushing over. This father already had a son at Choate. For his senior year, Evan was what you call a "prefect." A prefect is a senior in a house of either freshman or sophomores. Evan was living at Woodhouse with sophomores. The father literally gave me a hug and said, "Evan has *so* helped my son. His grades are up as Evan has taught him how to study. He's working out and looks and feels so much better. I don't know what my son would have done this year without him. All I hear from him is 'Evan said this' and 'Evan said that.' He has done so much for my son."

Only one word can describe how it made me feel—*proud*!

Baba, I hope you know I mean that.

Chapter 19
IT'S BIGGER THAN YOURSELF

CONFESSION—*I believe in angels.*

When I landed at Michigan, I realized collegiate gymnastics was not about just you, but many things much larger than you. Not only were you a part of *the team*, you were also a part of the whole Michigan athletics department—athletes, coaches, trainers, everyone. I quickly realized I was also a part of what I will call the team "family," which includes your family, your teammates' families and some very special people, even some you never met. Let me share a few examples.

Chip Hills

Chip Hills was the father of one of my teammates, Cailee. I never had the privilege of meeting him but was instantly impacted and moved by his family and the lessons they provided. It may sound odd to feel connected to a man I never met, but I will explain why. Here are some facts. I joined Michigan as a part of Team 40, the fortieth team in Michigan gymnastics history. Cailee, a year older, was part of Team 39. Team 39 had the advantage of having Chip Hills at every competition, either home or away, when they were in action. At the same time, he was fighting his own battle.

Chip was diagnosed with stage 4 pancreatic cancer with a five-year survival rate of 1 percent and was given six weeks to live. Instead of falling into sadness by the news, Chip and the rest of the Hills family devoted their time to doing things together that made them happy. One of those things was attending Michigan gymnastics meets to watch Cailee and the rest of Team 39. His love for the sport of gymnastics and the "spirited" traditions made him feel much more passionate about Michigan competitions. He did not miss a single meet. Regardless of the aggressive treatment he was receiving and the unpleasant side effects, he was there. I hear he was there always smiling and cheering.

During his battle, Chip lived by the motto of the North Carolina football team, the Panthers, which is "Keep Pounding." From the minute he was diagnosed, that became his motto for each and every day.

When Team 39 qualified for the national championship, something I got to do twice in my career, Mr. Hills wrote them a very special letter. In the letter, he expresses how proud he was of the girls for fighting their own battles and qualifying to Nationals. He expressed how the team's success helped him push through every day of chemo. Although the letter was addressed to Team 39, Bev got it engraved on a glass plaque to place in our team locker room. She wants every gymnast who comes through this program to understand how special Chip and his family are to our ever-changing Michigan family. It is the first thing you see when you walk into the locker room for practice and serves as a reminder. Your day may "suck," but "Keep Pounding." His signature is even on the plaque.

Chip, his wife, Debi, and their three girls, Lindsey, Brittany, and Cailee, would end each night by addressing three good things which happened that day. At my first meet as a freshman, Debi shared this anecdote with us. I distinctly remember her saying, some days, they could come up with twenty-five good things. Other days, just the sun coming up was where it began and ended. I've never forgotten that, and I truly learned to live by following the same mentality Chip and his family had.

He had another expression I hold dear—"Win the Day." Each day, you had to have a win, and again, it could be as simple as a great cup of coffee or a short supportive, email, text, or phone call from a friend to let him know they were thinking of him. He thought of it as a "win."

At this same first freshman year meet, the whole team wore a tattoo in the shape of a purple ribbon, symbolizing pancreatic cancer awareness on the base of our neck. On top of the ribbon were the words "Flip for Chip." For all four years of competition, Chip Hills and his special power was on the base of my neck. I just realized this, and it is something I am very proud of.

When I tore my Achilles my junior year, I wanted to sob. I wanted to lock myself in my room and live in denial. Minutes after I was carried into the locker room after hearing my Achilles pop (I know, it's gross, but it is what happened), I realized how stupid I was being. How could I complain about a silly foot surgery when Mr. Hills fought through cancer with a smile on his face and a love for life? I had to change my mentality.

I never would have approached my injury the same had it not been for Mr. Hills's inspiration. I made a promise to Bev, myself, and him as I lay on the training room table. I would not let this situation, and the fact my competition season was over bring me down. I would go through surgery and rehab and always, "Keep Pounding."

I am proud to share I was awarded the Chip Hills spirit award by the Hills family at our annual banquet at the end of my junior year. I'm the third recipient and my bestie, Emma was the fourth. Upon receiving the plaque, Cailee and her mother both leaned over to me and said, "He would have adored you. We just know it." Originally, I didn't bring a single medal or trophy to New York. I didn't feel the need or the attachment. That was then. This is now as I recently had a quick trip home, and I did bring this plaque back to my NYC pad and put it in my small (this is New York) living room. I find myself frequently looking at it and remembering Chip's fight and Cailee's and Debi's words.

Also, during my freshman year, I was a part of the first ever "Flip for Chip" meet. For this particular competition, the parents and any team fans wear a purple shirt with the words, "We Flip for Chip." I'm happy to say that I have four of these shirts. I'm also happy to share that for those specific four meets during my time at Michigan, he wasn't just on my neck; he was also on my shoulder. I made a promise to myself, and my dad and mom agreed. Each year, we will return for this special meet to celebrate him and his simple, powerful, and insightful message with the Hills family.

Together, we will "Flip for Chip," "Keep Pounding," and "Celebrate the Win." And of course, "Go Blue!"

Anna Abrams

Anna Abrams was another inspiration. She was thirteen and has cerebral palsy. She also has a great love of gymnastics. "Team Impact" is a national nonprofit that connects children facing serious and chronic illnesses with local college athletic teams. Fortunately, Anna was paired with us my senior year and became a ray of sunshine who came into the gym every week on Wednesdays. At home meets, Anna also got to come out on the floor with us in a Michigan gymnastics warmup jacket, "M" decal on the right side of her cheek, and hair braided. She would be right there on the floor cheering for each of us as a part of the team. I can see her big smile right now. She became a constant reminder to us: the simple joys are what really matter. We could compete. She could not. Yet, she was as much a part of the team as everyone else.

I never told Anna this, but hugging her after a floor routine (which you know is an important ritual for me) my senior year brought me such joy. It was so special because she was so special. And she made me feel special since we shared this experience together, competitor and spectator, yet teammates.

Anna Abrams, you were and are still an inspiration. Some days, your hug was my "win."

Chapter 20
THE BAD MAN AND BUBBLES

CONFESSION—*I wanted to drop out of school after my junior year in college. —Emma McLean.*

This next issue is rough, really rough. Most likely you have heard about the horrible, abominable behavior of Dr. Larry Nassar. According to Wikipedia, "Lawrence Gerard Nassar is an American convicted serial child molester who was the USA Gymnastics national team doctor and a former osteopathic physician at Michigan State University." I simply refer to him as "the monster."

During my freshman year of high school, I had a scheduled appointment with him for my back. We were willing to travel to East Lansing, Michigan from Chicago because of his reputation and masterful ability to get gymnasts, both male and female, back in action. Thankfully my mom was able to get an earlier appointment with a very gifted physician here in Chicago, Ellen Casey.

JIM INTERJECTION: I don't know how and why Olivia dodged this situation. As I wrote, I'm not a religious person. I can't thank some higher power for looking after her. I can just say we got lucky.

Unfortunately, many of my teammates and many of my fellow competitors didn't get so lucky. We're only estimating and could be wrong, but Dad and I believe somewhere between 60–70 percent of the gymnasts I know were affected by his aberrant, abusive, disgusting behavior. For some, I've learned it was many, many times over many, many years.

Back in 2015, two freshmen joined the gymnastics team, Emma McLean and me. We became instantly inseparable. Sophomore year she became my housemate for the next three years. She was my sidekick, and I was hers. A number of commentators and even our parents have actually confused us, as we look so alike from behind. Dave Kuzara, our assistant coach for two years, gave us the nickname, "Team Bubs," which ultimately morphed into my nickname for her—"Bubbles."

Emma saw Nassar for approximately six years prior to her tenure at Michigan. To be clear, once you join a collegiate athletic team, you are under their team medical supervision. You don't go elsewhere. Emma had many issues that Nassar skillfully fixed, briefly (she shared with me), including shoulder dislocations midway through a flip or giant on the high bar and frequently struggling when her arms gave out with no warning. Talk about dangerous. Nassar makes me sick, but he knew his shit, or at least he knew how to make it seem that he did.

In fact, Emma used to attribute much of her success and her Michigan scholarship to Nassar. In September 2016, Emma and I are beginning our sophomore year. I specifically remember Bev read an article out loud to Emma, on vault, and me, on beam, about the accusations.

She directly asked Emma since she knew she was a patient of his before coming to Michigan.

"Had you ever experienced this 'treatment?'"

"No, he would never do that. All he ever tried to do was help us."

I remember seeing her face, and she looked shocked and confused about why anyone would question him and his reputation.

Confessions of a **DIVISION-I ATHLETE**

I knew Emma for two years before landing at Michigan through club competitions in Region 5 (remember, that included Illinois and Michigan) and the Liukin Cup (which FYI, again, was a BFD). We started to get closer as we knew we were headed to the same place. During our freshman and sophomore years at Michigan, I got to know her like the back of my hand. We lived together. We trained together. We ate together. We competed together. We frequently roomed together.

Fast forward to the summer of 2017, as we are about to enter our junior year, and Nassar pleads guilty to federal child pornography charges. The community becomes more inquisitive. Could this be true? On November 22, 2017, he pleaded guilty to seven charges of first-degree sexual assault. This was the tipping point. Many began to realize, the "treatment" was not really a treatment.

I remember Emma telling me that the girls would stand in the locker room at her club gym and say, "Did he do the weird treatment to you?" She said this started around ages twelve to thirteen. They knew it was weird, but didn't have any frame of reference as *so* many of them were seeing Nassar, and you have to understand, you really don't have friends outside of the gym as you spend all your free time at the gym. You had no one else to ask.

Plus, many of Nassar's "patients" were doing well. Why would they question his techniques and treatments?

Emma returned from Thanksgiving break after this news a different person. Emma is spunky, funny, and an uber positive person. You feel it when you are around her. She comes from a terrific family. She's one of four. They're solid. Leah and Steve McLean raised four unique, strong, confident kids. Who stood before me after the holiday weekend and the news wasn't Emma. The infectious energy was gone.

On December 10, we had a party at our house. We all got dressed up and after the party planned on going out. Emma's usual "life of the party" personality was nowhere to be seen. I suspected this emotion and her changed demeanor was related to the accusations and the reality. He did it. He admitted it. Given how well I knew Emma and observed this change in her personality and the number of years she told me she was treated by him, I knew he had done it to her.

Bubbles never directly told me about Nassar. She didn't need to tell me. She knew me well enough to know I knew.

In January 2018 our junior year competition season was in full swing. It also coincided with the beginning of the Nassar trials.

The entire gymnastics community was either physically in court or tuning in on the live stream. Full disclosure, I spent all of my classes during this week with my computer open. I was obsessed with watching the empowerment of the survivors and frankly, watching this man suffer. Sadly, I had known many of the women standing up to speak since I was a little girl. We are a pretty small community. It was painful to watch, but I needed to watch because this is my sport and these are my "sisters," even if we have never met. It didn't matter. We were all going through this tragedy together.

A few days after the trials had begun, Bubbles came into my room downstairs.

"Livvie," she began. She always calls me that. "I have a question for you."

I looked up from my computer while doing homework to see her standing there. She looked both a little freaked out but still with an air of confidence. Something was up.

"Will you come to the trials with me? I think I want to speak."

Without hesitation I replied, "I'd be honored."

We woke up bright and early the next day and headed off to East Lansing.

We parked her car and walked to the front of the courthouse in the blistering Michigan cold. As we turned the corner, we saw Emma's parents, Leah and Steve, also relatively calm. Then we saw a line of people holding signs, "We Believe You—#MeToo."

Emma personally edited the contents of this chapter. She allowed me to share this fact; she only told her parents about her involvement in this situation a few weeks before the trial.

We walked into the packed courtroom, and immediately I felt sick. I can't imagine how Emma felt as I truly wanted to throw up when I saw his face. Judge Rosemary Aquilina brilliantly had the courtroom set up so Nassar was forced to face the whole courtroom as one by one, each survivor (FYI, there were some men as well; this man had *no* boundaries) went up to share their story and give their statement. After each testimony, the judge took up to five minutes to commend each person for their bravery and ability to stand before this courtroom and the monster and speak their truth.

I vividly remember watching Emma take a deep breath as she finally realized she was not alone. On this particular day, she took a lot of deep breaths. We all did.

Due to the influx of survivors wishing to share their story, Emma wasn't able to share hers with me by her side. We had to head back to Ann Arbor to make the 1:00 p.m. bus to Champaign, Illinois, for a meet the next day. As true employees of the University of Michigan, we went out there and did our job. It wasn't pretty and was the lowest team score we were ever a part of during our tenure at Michigan, but we came out with a win.

She did end up going back to court with her parents the next week and had her day in court. At that time, she wasn't publicly out as a survivor, so the live stream didn't broadcast her name, face, or voice. She shared her speech, out loud the night before, so I knew what she was going to say as I watched. I had a test and couldn't be there in person, but I was there for her in spirit. Because of anonymity, they kept the camera on Nassar. He cried the whole time she spoke.

The whole Nassar situation was truly painful to accept because it framed our junior year. There was a dark cloud looming over the gymnastics community during the entire 2018 competition season. No one understood how this man could correct injuries and give young athletes the opportunity to continue to train and compete in a sport they loved. He gave them back their sport and, as we have written, their identity. At the same time he gave, boy did he take. For some, he took their innocence. For some, he took their self-confidence and self-esteem. For some, this horrible man ingrained ongoing PTSD from what he did to them while continuing in their sport.

And for many, he just *took* their sport. Yes, some quit rather than even have the slightest chance they would have to see him again, endure him again, and be treated by him, again.

A quick anecdote—The team collaborates and decides which leotard best suits each competition. Sometimes it's a no-brainer; sometimes there is tension. You had to be strategic, given the colors of the competition. For example, when we compete at Alabama (their colors are red and white), we make sure to wear a very vibrant and Michigan "in your face" leotard. We have an odd leotard that is entirely metallic silver. When the team put it on, we all looked like kitchen appliances. It is not flattering and regardless of your size, you look like a big box of brushed stainless steel. Bev happens to love this leo because she finds it unique. She wouldn't find it so "unique" if she had to wear it.

We escaped this leo junior year since our seniors at the time hated it and blatantly refused to wear it. But Bev is no dummy. She knew it was there in the apparel closet just waiting to be worn. So we knew we had to take one for the team. Therefore, we were destined to be traumatized by it senior year. Knowing our fate, we choose to dress in the "Kitchen Aid" leos at our in-house mock competition, the intrasquad I mentioned before, so less people would see us as flying Frigidaires.

After about fifty jokes and comments from the team, centered around our keen resemblance to oven doors, Emma's always positive attitude said, "Well, we look like steel, but you can't break steel!" That instantly became our motto for our final, senior year. We even have silver bracelets with the inscription "Can't Break Steel." My dad actually wears mine sometimes because he says he can feel its power.

During the Nassar situation, Emma was our steel. No matter how many times she must have thought about it or was asked a question about it, she stayed strong. Amazingly strong. As awful as everything about this situation is and was, I believe Emma taught me a new level of caring for myself, mentally and physically.

JIM INTERJECTION: This section makes me both sick to my stomach and enraged. I love Emma. She's like a daughter. I can't begin to imagine what she and so many others went through at the time and have to process and live with now as adults.

Don't forget, a gymnast's career literally swings from one injury to another. Think for a moment, the horrible feeling when you realize you have hurt yourself. You hear the pop (Olivia did when she blew her Achilles) or feel the pain and then the thought has to cross your mind, "Why did this happen?" Did I make a silly mistake or was this coming on for some time? You are already upset, in pain and experiencing some degree of trauma.

Now add in, "OMG, now I have to go see Nassar" and suffer a second unknown and/or unexpected or expected trauma. Possibly a series of Nassar traumas since most injuries don't get corrected and repaired with one treatment. That's why we wrote that he treated injuries, "briefly." Did they ignore and live with the pain to avoid him? Did they ask to see another physician instead? Did they ever ask him why he was doing this weird treatment? Emma told me he would explain the theory and background of the "treatment." Given his position and status in the gymnastics community, naïve young gymnasts didn't think to question him. Shocking. It is astonishing these young women and men could then get back up on an apparatus, multiple apparatus, to train and compete. Compete where perfection is the goal. How do you compartmentalize these emotions and facts? Nothing short of astonishing.

FACT: Many of these "treatments" occurred behind a pulled curtain while the parents were actually in the room. Additional fact: As with many addicts, the level of his abuse had to escalate to give him the same high. Plus, the frequency also had to increase so he would do this many, many times a day. It wasn't "one and done." It was more like "all day and done."

Nassar was first accused of inappropriate behavior in 1997, two decades before the situation blew up. Allegedly, more than enough people knew what he was up to yet stayed quiet. This may allegedly include the Michigan State Athletic Department and possibly the individuals in charge of the Olympic training center in Walker County, Texas. This has led to many, many "resignations," and a considerable amount of damage to the school, USA Gymnastics, and the Olympic training center. This included both reputational and financial damage. Good. How disgusting to know this was going on, only to stay silent.

I'm going to throw the conclusion of this chapter to Emma and Olivia, who wrote this together:

As awful as it was to write and relive, it's true, you "can't break steel." No, we don't want to ever put those leos on again, and Bev, please spare future teammates from the trauma. We are strong, confident women, women who can compete, fall, break things, tear things, and face plant more than we would like to remember. We can lose *and* win. We can also overcome overwhelming obstacles, like this one, by leaning on each other and holding each other up. We joined a team. We are a team. We always will be a team.

We would like to end this chapter with direct quotes from some of the brave survivors:

"Little girls don't stay little forever. They grow into strong women who return to destroy your world." —Kyle Stephens, the first one to speak at the trial and a former Nassar family friend.

"We are now a force and you are nothing." —Aly Raisman, 2012 and 2016 Olympic gold medal winner.

"I didn't quit after my junior year. My senior year was the *best* redemption I could have asked for." —Emma McLean.

Chapter 21
A DAD AND DAUGHTER'S GUIDE TO SURVIVING BODY IMAGE (PART 1)

CONFESSION—*It's never been as bad as it is now.*

My next chapter began immediately post gymnastics. I went through the post athletic period where I realized my body wasn't owned by anyone anymore. I've talked with my friends, many former D-I athletes, said they now feel the same.

A school didn't own my weight.

A sport didn't own my weight.

A coach didn't own my weight.

I had never felt so free before.

Right after we lost in the semi-final of the national championships in Fort Worth, Texas, we were sad. No, not true. First, there was a rush of happiness as you realize you don't have to go through the stress of competing the next day. Then the sadness took over. I haven't cried yet. I still haven't had my major "I'm actually done with gymnastics" cryfest, but Emma, the team, and I definitely were sad. In an attempt to cheer us up the next day, someone said, "Let's hit an In-N-Out Burger," mentioned earlier as a special reward since they are mostly on the West Coast.

I've never been a big burger girl. I don't usually go somewhere and order a burger. I've just never loved them enough to scope out the best place to get one. For some odd reason, after our loss, In-N-Out sounded like the bomb.

First In–N–Out. Next, pizza! Couple days later? Fries. When the bread and butter arrived at the table I thought, "Let's hit that too." Then the biggest gift of all? A whopping fifteen extra pounds.

And depression.

JIM'S INTERJECTION: It's hard to put a number on the total calories Olivia burned during practice, lift (which was twice a week before school for an hour, and Sundays at noon, and that's weight lifting, FYI), and competition, where the adrenaline alone amps up your metabolism and burns a ton of calories. It had to be thousands upon thousands of calories each week. To give you a frame of reference, for a 120-pound person, he or she would burn around sixty to seventy calories when walking a mile; a 180-pound person would be closer to one hundred calories. Of course, this all depends on how fit you are because a person in better shape would actually burn less calories since their heart and circulatory system are more efficient. That's how I come to the conclusion that Olivia and her teammates burned so many calories.

Also, as some of you who know me would already know, muscle burns more calories than fat. Therefore, the number of calories these talented gymnasts burned each day, even if they just lay down all day, would be significantly higher, given their muscle to fat ratio.

I found myself looking in the mirror before going to bed, wishing the weight would just disappear in the middle of the night. As depressed as I was about my weight and how I looked, I couldn't 100 percent commit to getting rid of it. Plus, we told you what my dad does for a living. Mr.

Weight Loss. Mr. Fitness Expert. Mr. Perfect. He never is out of shape. He doesn't gain weight. I'm bumping into his friends and clients every time I walk down the street. Lucky me. Ugh!

During this time, post-graduation, I was with my dad almost 100 percent of the time as he lives in downtown Chicago, where I was raised. In 2018, my mom moved to the suburbs. I rarely eat in front of my dad. I've come to learn this is a common theme from many people when he's around. He doesn't make us feel this way by what he says or does. Internally, we just feel the pressure.

We recently went to dinner at a new hot restaurant with Evan, my dad, Whitney, one of dad's besties, and her two sons. It's super loud and crowded. Service is spotty as the place is pretty new. The night is not off to a great start.

Then the ordering begins. Ceviche. Quinoa and tuna salad—which we then found out they were out of. Sharable plate of pork shank (my dad didn't touch it), listed to serve two to three people, and Shishito peppers. When the first Ceviche arrived, it was a small plate with four pieces of fish the size of quarters, which we cut in half since there were six of us. Took about two seconds to finish. Evan, being a pig, soon realizes this restaurant serves portions that are truly the definition of "small plates," and announces, "Every man for himself."

I don't know why, but after a few bites I turn to my dad and say, "I've been working out a lot and feel pretty good. Have I lost any weight?"

He puts his hand on mine and says, "Let's talk about that later." Immediately the tears started to well up. I quickly headed to the bathroom for a good cry.

JIM INTERJECTION: Whitney looks at me and says, "What just happened?" and I tell her what she asked and what I said, and she says, boldly gesturing, "You idiot. LIE!" and jumps up to follow Olivia into the bathroom.

Whitney finds me hiding in one of gender neutral, individual bathrooms and brings me into a private corner away from the bathroom traffic.

"Olivia, you are a beautiful, young woman who does not need to be told anything about weight. Do not let this affect you because you are bigger than your weight."

I pulled myself together, and we both went back to the table.

After not one, but two rounds of ample food orders, my dad says the unimaginable:

"Is it just me, or is everyone starving?"

Whitney pipes up without missing a beat, "Really, this from a man who eats a Tic Tac for dinner."

This line is now a part of Karas vocabulary. We have taken it so far as to differentiate what color Tic Tac applies to which meal, breakfast, lunch, or dinner.

I'm struggling. I have this routine, as many girls know. When I'm putting my pants on, I do some squats and try to hike them up. My dad was in the kitchen, and my room is right next door. On my second squat I hear a loud sound. It's a rip. I have completely split the back seem of my favorite white jeans. I was horrified to tell him. Then I hear:

"Is everything okay in there?"

Silence. He walks in my room and sees the tears.

Then just last night I broke a strap off of my favorite summer dress. WTF.

I am only doing cardio, core, and stretching. This muscle *has* to come off my body. Haven't touched a weight. Haven't even hung from a bar. My lats, my back muscles, remain huge and don't seem to realize I'm not getting back on bars. I don't need these lats. My dad explains, given a decade and a half of conditioning, and muscle memory, and they are *still* hanging on waiting for me to once again hang on and swing from the bars.

Here is my present strategy:

1. Don't force myself to workout. Do it when I want to and therefore get more out of it. If my head is not into it, it will feel forced, I will feel pissed, and it will be a waste of time since I won't work very hard. It will probably make me eat more. If I want to do it, then I generally put way more effort into it and therefore get more out of it.
2. Eat slower. This is what Toni, my petite, Italian grandmother, always told me when I was younger, and she would watch me scarf down a big plate of carbs, carbs and sugar after practice."
3. Recognize what a "good" full is.
4. Cool it with the Hot Tamales. The breakup was rough, but the Tamales understood. We couldn't "just be friends." We needed a clean split.
5. Be mindful.

It's starting to work. It won't happen overnight, but like the beam, I can fall off and get right back up and, once again, persevere. I'm going to make my weight my bitch. I'm just not there yet.

JIM INTERJECTION: I have said this to clients for many, many years. Don't let the number on the scale determine who you are and how you treat and respect yourself. Now, I'm not condoning a high weight or a significant amount of weight gain. I'm really speaking to a group who abuse themselves emotionally over ten or fifteen or twenty extra pounds. No, you are most likely not going to get back to your wedding weight. Please don't show me a picture in your cheerleading uniform when you were all hurling with regularity to stay so ridiculously thin. Also, don't tell me about when you were captain of the basketball team at Duke and wore size 31 jeans. Tell me about today. Let's do something about your situation, now, and together let's make a plan.

Pick a weight. If you feel you are up twenty, then shoot to get ten off and then flatline it. By "flatlining it," I mean get there and stay there. Don't yo-yo wildly. Yes, do get on the scale every day. The research agrees since the scale doesn't lie. I recently said this on a radio interview and a listener called in and told me I was shaming them by telling them to get on the scale.

Okay, don't get on the scale. Try another strategy. I have one: jeans. Once a week, ideally on a Saturday or Sunday, put on a pair of nonstretch jeans that once fit. If they fit, bravo. If they don't, keep them on, all day. Remind yourself, "I don't think I was following my plan." Don't take them off and get comfortable. Get comfortable feeling uncomfortable. This isn't a punishment. It's a reality check.

My strategy with Olivia right now is just shut up. We leave for Aspen in a few weeks for the holiday season. Olivia has never been on skis as she was never allowed by a coach in case of an injury. This is her time, the first time she has the opportunity to choose how she spends her time. Then she flies back to New York with Baba on January 4th. I'm going to trust her ability to figure this whole weight and body image issue out on her own, and I'm certainly *not* going to pressure her. When she needs me, I'm a text, phone call, or flight away. She knows I'm in her corner. I just need to get out of that ring and let her punch it out on her own.

Chapter 22
A DAD AND DAUGHTER'S GUIDE TO SURVIVING BODY IMAGE (PART 2)

CONFESSION—*I'm a former fatty father with issues.*

As I said in the introduction, this book was going to be different. It wasn't supposed to be another book about weight loss and body image. Somehow, by default, now it is. I'm not going to fight it.

You know what I do for a living. What you don't know, except for my quick reference in the introduction, is how I struggled with my weight and body image in the past. Every now and then, I still do.

I have a routine. I get out of the shower every morning and take a quick inventory:

Face? Doesn't look puffy or fat today.

Abs? I've never had definition, but when I'm at my fighting weight, they are pretty flat.

Turn to the side and look at my midsection? As I just turned sixty, yes, even I have seen an increase, a thickening, in my midsection. It's not visible from the front, but it's right there from the side. I can tell from this angle, *and* from my face if I'm up in weight.

So, the next time I am at my studio I get on the *same* scale. I think I'm up from my inventory. Yep, the scale agreed.

Let's get this weight off or I am going to start that slow creep up in weight that many reading may be nodding their heads about.

Here's some personal history:

As a little boy, I vividly remember my mother asking me, "Did you have your ice cream of the day?"

The truth: "Yes, I ate it before breakfast"

The lie: "Not yet, Mom."

If you want a good laugh, check out this video of Baby's first ice cream. Clearly that was me—https://www.youtube.com/watch?v=9ClrpO-r-LM

I was always on a diet, desperately trying to lose weight. Not much success. In my teens, I tried the "smoking" diet. Smoke for breakfast, lunch, and dinner. Also, before and after breakfast, lunch, and dinner. It worked until food was around. Then, it didn't. My weight finally topped out around 220 my sophomore year in college. It wasn't pretty.

I spent many nights in the living room of my fraternity house, "The Castle," in the middle of Penn's campus. I would eat potato chips—Charles Chips—which were delivered in a one-pound tin (virtually nothing was delivered back then but pizza and these chips) and drink Gallo Chablis out of the jug. I did this while watching *Dynasty*, as my goal was to become the next Blake Carrington, but I'm saving these stories for another book.

To this day, if someone says, "Let's go to the pool or beach," I still suffer post-traumatic stress disorder. I'm once again a shirtless, chubby boy with a pot belly who looked like crap. Then add, my parents and grandparents who would say, "Doesn't Tzimmy (the Greek pronunciation of Jimmy, my childhood nickname) have a cute potbelly." Three mistakes:

1. Never bring attention to something that clearly is *not* cute as cute.
2. Never call out a child's, or anyone's, body image. I knew the potbelly was there. I'm not dumb.
3. Tzimmy? Really?

I know what it feels like to struggle. Many of the experts in my field share a common denominator: we all struggled. It's painful. There is an empathy we share for something probably 75 percent of the American population shares—too much weight, or cargo as Olivia calls it. The word *cargo* kills me. My baby had to find another word for too much weight.

For thirty-three years, it has been my job to help my clients, readers, and followers overcome their obstacles and issues. I keep thinking, *How can I help others but watch my daughter struggle? What have I done wrong?*

I knew my profession could pop an issue with my kids. As Olivia wrote, she didn't know what a calorie was because it was never discussed. I also knew her sport had the potential to pop an issue. I knew Olga did not place an emphasis on weight. She didn't have to with Olivia who, prior to puberty, was a stick.

I did see her body quickly change with puberty. I didn't know how difficult the challenge has been and definitely didn't know about the high school bulimia. The fact I missed the bulimia haunts me. I know how to check. You look under the toilet seat. When you toss, it splashes back up and I have seen it many times in other toilets, but never in one of mine.

I do know about the struggles at Michigan, but I didn't know to what degree. Now, I see it every time we are together, whether in Chicago or at her apartment in New York.

I see the pain on Olivia's face when she tries to talk about her weight or wants my response to what she has been trying to do to bring it down. I stupidly brought it up once. Big mistake! She left her command position in tears. It breaks my heart.

Just a few months ago, we had lunch with a mentor of mine, Michael Clemente. Michael was the executive producer of *World News Tonight* back in the Peter Jennings days and went on to be the executive producer of the cable channel, ABC *News Now*. Back in 2004, he gave me my show, *Couch Potatoes*, which I loved hosting. Years later we both moved on, but we still stay in touch. I wanted him to meet Olivia and, of course, he offered to help her in her job search.

Olivia told me about this interchange, when I got up to go to the bathroom, Michael said, "I love seeing your dad. But it's always so hard to see your dad . . ." because Michael, like many, many people, is working on his weight.

"Oh really, try being his daughter."

"Okay, worse."

Michael agreed. As a newsman always looking for the truth, he knew it when he heard it.

Another current challenge is Baba. He's a tall string bean we call "The Insect." He can eat whatever he wants, whenever he wants. But, in his defense for all the eating, he works out a lot. He's not just genetically gifted, which is very, *very* rarely the case. He's on it. He works his own program, even though he eats me out of house and home. Buy five pounds of grapes? The next afternoon, "Dad, we need grapes."

I have eating and body weight issues. The way people say, "I'm a recovering alcoholic," I can honestly say, "I'm a recovering chubby boy." Have I recovered completely? No. Did I pass this on to Olivia?

God, I hope not.

But I think I did.

Chapter 23
THE GOOD, THE NOT-SO-GOOD, AND THE REALLY BAD

CONFESSION—*Read on:*

I've shared a lot of history, stories, situations, and people. I thought I would just take a moment to give you a quick walk down my Michigan memory lane. I've put it in simple categories as referenced in the title.

I need to be clear—there are two big championships each year in Women's Collegiate Gymnastics at Michigan:

1. The Big Ten championship. Only ten schools compete, and I have to give you a heads up: Michigan won all four years I was there.
2. NCAA championships. My first three years, twelve teams qualified. In 2019, my senior year, the rules changed, and only eight teams qualified. That is what makes my final NCAA Nationals so very special.

Here's a rundown.

Freshman Year
The Good

New, exciting, fun, loved the upperclassmen. Emma and I are becoming besties and are the well-taken-care-of babies.

A crazy record bar rotation at Regionals, the 9.95 after 9.95 after 9.95 after 9.95, which we told you about before.

First Big Ten championship win.

Won Big Ten freshman of the year.

The Not So Good

Fell on the beam at Regionals. You know the story.

The Really Bad

The removal of a very toxic teammate who lived with the sophomores and was truly just a terrible person. She refused to medically retire (yes, she had issues and a lot of them) and give the scholarship back to us to enable the team to have one more capable competitor. Bad decision.

Sophomore Year
The Good

We matched a Michigan school gymnastics record by achieving a 197.825 total score out of a possible 200 at our "Flip for Chip" meet. As I said before, something special about Chip Hills and his amazing character gave us super powers at those meets.

However, I am happy (but sad I wasn't a part of it) to report the new Michigan Women's Gymnastics record is a 197.95, achieved on February 22, 2020.

I placed fifth on vault at NCAA Nationals.

I became an All American because I placed fifth on vault at NCAA Nationals. The top ten competitors on each event at Nationals achieve this honor.

Second Big Ten championship win.

Emma landed a 9.975 on her vault at the Big Ten championship.

I won the Big Ten floor title.

The Not So Good

A bad, toxic breakup with a fellow athlete, who also happened to be besties with a lot of my best friends. Tough.

We competed at Ohio State, our biggest rival. After completing my floor routine, I made the Michigan "M," where you make your fingers look like an "M." Extend your thumbs and touch the tips together, then extend both index fingers and point them down. I pointed it right at the student section and was promptly booed off the floor. My first boo but not my last.

JIM INTERJECTION: Olivia needed a car, so I took her shopping. I saw a really cool red Honda CRV.

"Honey, what do you think about that one. The red is super cool."

"Are you insane?"

"No. I think it's really cute."

"Do you want me to get killed?"

"No, why would a car get you killed?"

"It's red, Dad. That's the Ohio State's color."

"Oh, who cares about that."

"I do!"

A red car was not purchased. Once again, clueless. That's why this landed in "The Not So Good" category.

Emma was robbed on her vault. I call BS on the 9.975. It was a 10!

The Really Bad

Team dynamic, it was just bad—cliques, hatred, and a lot of negative vibes. I really don't want to go into it because it would require naming names, and I don't feel, in this instance, that would be the right thing to do. Just know it was bad.

Junior Year
The Good

At the sixth meet of the season, at Crisler, the Big Ten commentators were all over my floor routine saying, "This could be Olivia Karas's much-deserved perfect 10."

Third Big Ten championship win.

Bev's twenty-third Big Ten championship win, tying the Big Ten record. This is for *all* sports, not just gymnastics. Bev tied *the* record!

I won two very special awards:

- The Big Ten Sportsmanship Award, presented just to me, in a boot from my Achilles surgery and
- The Chip Hills Spirit Award—very special!

The Not So Good

I land my final tumbling pass on my hands and knees.

The Really Bad

Tore my right Achilles. Bye-bye "10." Hello surgery.

The Nassar trials.

Jim Plocki, Bev's husband, battles leukemia.

Senior Year
The Good

The absolute best team, best team dynamic, camaraderie, genuine friendships, great energy, and respect.

Winning our fourth Big Ten championship.

Bev's twenty-fourth Big Ten championship win, breaking the Big Ten record. Once again, this is for *all* sports, not just gymnastics. Bev now holds *the* record!

Qualifying for Nationals over the University of Alabama at Regionals. The amazing win with my ugly crying.

Finishing fifth in the nation as a team at the NCAA championships. Jim Plocki beats leukemia.

The Not So Good

Maggie tore her Achilles (copycat!).

Emma broke her hand the day before we left for Nationals. We lost two incredibly valuable soldiers.

Missing the final round of Nationals as we needed Emma and Maggie but did do the best we could without them.

Figuring out something was up with a coach and both a housemate and teammate. I knew something was up, and when I confronted her, she blasted me and said the vilest things to me. I didn't want to be right. Unfortunately, I was.

The Really Bad

As I mentioned: A coach. My housemate and teammate. A car in a mall parking lot at 9:00 a.m. Steamed up windows. Dual arrests.

The fallout from the above-mentioned incident. It permeated my house, my team, our collective emotional state, my school, everything.

Chapter 24
KKG

CONFESSION—*Sorry KKG, this isn't Kappa Kappa Gamma.*

It's Kappa Kappa Gymnastics.

I'm a Little Sister and Don't Even Know It

Before I got to Michigan, my future teammate, Tal, was taken under the wing of Remma Zakharia. Remma was a senior when Tal was a freshman. She has also done brilliant choreography for my team for a number of years. She knows how to showcase both our top talents and our personality. If you go to YouTube.com and watch my senior year floor routine, my personal favorite, that was all Remma. She believed Madonna, Frank Sinatra, and *High School Musical* defined me. Together, we blended the music and the moves and of all my career routines, hands down, this defined me both as a person and as a competitor. Remma, "thank you" for giving me this experience.

According to Tal, Remma and she instantly bonded, and Remma became what sororities call Tal's big sister. When I joined the team in 2015, Tal and I had a similar connection. I later learned she and Remma consulted and made the decision to add me to their lineage. Remma is Tal's big sister. Tal is the little sister. I'm the grand little sister, and Remma actually refers to me as "grand" in text messages or on the phone. As I look back, this was my first experience with this sisterhood, KKG.

JIM INTERJECTION: I believe in "Pay It Forward." Good deeds and actions come back to you. You don't do it for this reason. You do it because you believe it the right or the kind thing to do. As Olivia wrote in chapter 1, she moved to New York and posted it on Instagram. I have a love/hate relationship with social media, but this is a part of the love. Quite a few people within the gymnastics community, whether they knew her personally or not, reached out to welcome her to the city, invite her to have coffee, lunch, a drink, dinner, whatever. It was a great way for her to instantly feel connected to old and new friends and a new city.

The night after her meltdown in the command positions we wrote about in chapter 1, Olivia told me she was going out for drinks. Olivia's new BFF is Scott Bregman from the Olympic Channel, and a former Michigan gymnast. He's a blast as I've gotten to know him. Olivia said she invited a fellow gymnast she knows of, yet had never actually met, to join.

"Why?" I asked.

"People were so kind to me in New York. I wanted to do the same for her because I don't know if she knows a lot of people in Chicago."

Sydney Snead was a star gymnast at the University of Georgia and just graduated as well. Since Olivia was here for the weekend, she hit her up on Instagram to get together and introduce her to some Chicago friends, Scott included. They were all going to meet at a bar. I said, "Why don't you have Sydney over here to pre-game before meeting everyone else?" I thought it would be nice for them to have time to get to know one another as they had never actually met, never had a conversation face to face. But boy, did they know a lot about each other.

Fact 1: They competed about two dozen times against each other in club before college.

Fact 2: They competed six times against each other when they were at Georgia and Michigan.

As the dad, I assumed I would come out, say "hi," pour them a glass of wine, then hide in my bedroom and give them the living room to chat. From the moment Sydney walked in, it was literally like two old friends reconnecting. I poured Sydney her wine and sat down in the living room with Olivia to get to know her. OMG, what a fascinating conversation. Here are a few snippets.

"Olivia, am I wrong? Didn't you break your back at one point?"

"Yes, when I was in my freshman year of high school."

"I thought so. I did too. When I watched you compete at 2014 Nationals, I remember someone telling me you had broken yours."

NOTE: If you remember, we mentioned Sydney on page 104 as Olivia was looking up scores and locations for meets. There was her name at the level 10, 2014 Nationals in Long Beach, California. She was in the number two, all-around position, right behind Olivia at number one.

"And weren't we both at The Ranch, the Olympic training center in Texas (which recently closed down on account of the Nassar crap) at the same time?"

"Yes, we were."

"Wasn't that the worst experience ever?"

"Yes," Sydney said, "I called my mom and told her I wanted to come home early. It was just awful."

Olivia interjection: I only attended the ranch once since it is invitation only. Many girls have been there numerous times to train for the Olympics, but my invitation was a "one and done." And thank God for it. I felt a spooky vibe there, a vibe that I *assumed* would bring passion and drive as this place was considered the gymnastics mecca. It did quite the opposite. It was dark, silent, cold, and reeked of negative energy. All I can say is I found it, "No bueno!" and was thrilled to never go back.

A little later:

"I used to black out on the beam."

"So did I," said Sydney.

JIM INTERJECTION: This conversation occurred after we wrote Olivia confessed she was a beam "black outer." Now she came to realize, she wasn't alone. I wonder, how many current and former gymnasts, or any athletes for that matter, have blacked out while competing or playing their sport? I bet it's more than you imagine.

"Do you like X?" who was a well knows competitor, but not on either of their teams.

"OMG, what a nut job."

"I agree. Had to room with her once, and she is certifiable."

Meeting Other Queens

I watched Sam Peszek compete for years. She was one of my idols. She is an analyst for the PAC-12 Network and the host of her own podcast, "I Have Cool Friends." She also is the founder of Beam Queen Bootcamp I previously referenced, a two-day event entirely focused on mastering the beam, both mentally and physically. Sam invites other Olympians and NCAA stars to share their personal experience and strategy to shine.

After successfully making the beam my bitch, I wanted to get involved in this camp to share my journey. I texted Tal, who knew Sam from Aly Raisman within the Olympic gymnastics world, and we connected.

Before meeting her, she texted me and asked me to be on her "I Have Cool Friends" podcast on season two, highlighting NCAA gymnastics.

I thought, *One of my idols is asking* me *to be on her podcast?*

Heck yeah.

I have since helped coach Beam Queen bootcamp in both Colorado and Indiana. What is interesting about this specific bootcamp is that we all had to compete on beam. Yes, you also know I sucked, then sucked less. We had to compete on beam if you wanted to be considered for the all-around position. Yes, it does make a bit of a difference if you are an all-around competitor. You get a leg up. You receive more attention, both from the spectators and the commentators and clearly there is award potential, as you are up for a recognition many others are not. You are looked upon somewhat differently as you have mastered (let's hope) all four apparatus.

Look, in club, this sometimes determines who gets more attention from schools. It makes you more desirable if you can compete in all four events because you are carrying more of the load, the competition load, especially when you consider how injuries sideline so many competitors in certain events.

I have had numerous dinners and drinks with Sam since I moved to New York. We also try out wacky exercise classes together, then text about how our bodies feel the next day. Always on the hunt for fun, she spices it up by inviting her other peeps such as Katelyn Ohashi (remember her from scoring), Bridget Sloan, 2009 World All-Around champion with too many accolades to note (Love you, Bridget, but really, eight NCAA titles? Who are you?). Hallie Mossett, another UCLA gymnast who went viral for the Beyoncé routine and now is a professional choreographer and stunt double for everything media, movies, TV shows, you name it. Also Cory Tomlinson, who was the team manager for UCLA and owns his own business called Team Make It Loud.

Back in my club days, the top eight girls in each age group at Regionals qualify to Nationals. My junior year of high school at Regionals, I came in second in my age group to Bre Showers, who won the meet after landing her final beam dismount and tearing her ACL. Ufortunately, Bre couldn't then come to Mississippi and compete at Nationals (on second thought, maybe fortunate for me as if you remember, I won that meet). Bre and I have stayed in touch ever since as she's a doll. Bre was recruited by Oklahoma, the powerhouse school in gymnastics. Also joining her class was Maggie Nichols, who just missed qualifying for the 2016 Olympics. Needless to say Maggie came into NCAA gymnastics with a vengeance.

As Bre and I remained in touch, she then introduced me to Maggie, who, besides having twenty-two perfect 10s in her four years of college and being the recipient of the AAI Award (the Heisman of collegiate gymnastics) in 2020. Maggie is another amazing, strong, determined woman and I'm proud to call her a KKG sister.

Why do I drop all these names? Because when I was a little girl, I watched the 2008 Beijing Olympics and idolized Sam and Brigdet. Then I watched them in the NCAA and idolized them even more.

It isn't only social either. I was nominated by Bev to be an ambassador for a group called Collegiate Gymnastics Growth Initiative (CGGI). The group is spearheaded by former UCLA associate head coach, Randy Lane, and consists of ten former NCAA gymnasts. The group works to increase awareness of NCAA gymnastics and collegiate opportunitites. Be honest, when you think of a gymnast, don't the Olympics immediately pop into your mind as the end goal? There is another option many may not be aware of or fully understand. Members include Katelyn, McKenna Kelley, former Louisiana State University star gymnast, and me, but also many talented women from Cornell, Denver, Florida, Oklahoma, and California, some of whom I knew in the past and some who are now new friends from being part of this growth initiative.

It's also been fun to connect with other gymnasts through commentary, our new way of staying involved with the sport. I just had a blast working with McKenna when we covered a meet together in Missouri. Just like my Sydney story, McKenna and I immediately clicked and realized we had loads in common. Over "Skinny" margs after the meet, we literally had to be pried apart, or we would have stayed at it all night. McKenna, we *have* to work together again in the future.

Now, we all belong to KKG. No matter what school, what year, what degree of success. You joined. You may not know you joined, but you did.

We share a common thread of this sport defining who we are. We also share not having a life in high school, destroying our bodies, not joining a sorority (all but verboten for athletes at this level), and putting on an extra small leotard too many weekends to imagine. The pressure. The balance. The highs and lows. Without this sport, I never would have met these amazing women and had the opportunity to join this sorority.

Did I know this would happen? Absolutely not. You are probably tired of both my dad and me writing, "I had no clue," but truthfully, I had *no* clue this "sisterhood" would be so important in my post gymnastics life.

I can't wait to meet future sorority sisters.

Chapter 25
I HAVE B1G, "HUGE" NEWS

CONFESSION—*I thought I would never get a job.*

Some things in life, and some people in life, truly come full circle.

In my attempt to fill my void of gymnastics, void of Ann Arbor friends and void of job, I pursued many part-time positions, one being writing for *FloGymnastics*, a digital platform that shares all news gymnastics all the time. I was writing a piece on veteran and legendary coaches in the NCAA and, of course, first called Bev.

"How the job search coming along?" Oh boy, there's the squawk I now miss.

"It's fine. You know me, and I don't do well without structure. I've been trying to build my resume with part-time jobs and assignments like this one. Of course, I'm also going on interviews and networking, but nothing has stuck yet."

"What field do you want to work in again?"

"Marketing, communications, public relations, or broadcasting."

"Really? My former assistant coach was just in town. She is married to a guy who is very high up at a company in Brooklyn. I think they do what you want to do. Maybe he can help. Would you like me to connect you?"

"Absolutely. I would love nothing more."

As I previously wrote, Bev always has her phone in hand and glasses on top of her head, I'm sure the glasses instantly came down because in a moment, an email pops up introducing me to Raj Singhal, the COO and CFO at Huge. According to their homepage, "Huge is a full-service digital agency, who transforms brands and builds businesses."

November 14, 2019, I meet with Christie Giera-Allport, Managing Director of Global Communications at Huge. I'm totally nervous but try not to show it.

November 22, 2019, I meet with Carrie Cummings, also on the communications team, and skyped with Raj. Before the meeting, I purposely got on the Stairmaster, and yes, watched old gymnastics competition routines in order to calm my nerves and focus.

On December 7, 2019, my dad is in town as we are crashing this book, and we are both working out, independently, at a gym close to my New York pad. Okay, it's a little dirty, but my dad is cool as it's my gym and now my "jam." He knows I have a scheduled call at 10:00 a.m. with Huge. At 9:55 a.m., he texts me, "I have a really good feeling about this call. I think you are going to get offered a job." I didn't see it at the time.

At 10:05 on December 7, 2019, I was offered a job at Huge.

At 10:08 on December 7, 2019, I found my dad on the lat pulldown machine and silently walked in front of it so he could see me, mid rep. He saw my big eyes and let go of the high bar. It took a few seconds before I could get out, "I GOT A JOB." Neither of us spoke for close to a minute. I stood, he sat, both of us in tears.

On that same day, in the late afternoon, ten minutes after receiving a detailed email employment offer, I went over it with my dad—and I accepted.

I am a communications coordinator and will report directly to Christie.

I just have to write it again—I GOT A JOB!

It's the day after, and I'm still in shock. I start on Monday, January 6, so I have about a month to breathe, finish this book, and then hit the ground running.

As graduation was May 5, it took a total of seven months or 216 days, to land this job. But, it's Huge! And no, that joke will never get old. I feel fortunate but must be clear. I really tried to work every angle possible. Clearly, I got a lot of "no's" and "nothing available right now." But I'm telling anyone in the same place, use the Karas verb "persevere." Keep at it even though it sucks at the time being jobless. No one is going to come knocking on your front door and say, "You interested in a job?"

I've actually taken a deep breath. No, a very deep breath. I have a month to enjoy the holidays; as I have shared, I am Christmas crazy. Then, as my dad told you, Aspen to ring in the New Year, on skis. My "second" mom and second "second" mom would have lost it had they learned I was on skates or skis. I wanted to make them happy. I listened.

Now the slopes are calling me. I am absolutely horrified to put on a pair of skis and told my dad this fact. He said, "You can do a front and back flip on a beam, four inches wide, and can't put on skis? I think you will be great. You deserve this time. You deserve to get out of a rancid feet-smelling gym and breathe some fresh air."

My dad also wants you to know that he just got not one raise, but two! First, I go on Huge health insurance starting in February, so I'm off of his. Second, our deal was he would pay my rent my first year out of college. We also agreed, once I got a job, I would pay half the rent while also actively looking for a roommate to pay the other half. Dad and daughter are both happy—for now.

I also have another update.

My B1G news. I just signed a freelance agreement with the Big Ten Network to call gymnastics meets (FYI, the Big Ten is referred to as B1G for short, I'm pretty proud of this play on words...). Dean Linke, a well-known Big Ten network anchor, covers many sports, gymnastics included. During my four years of college, Dean and I got to know each other well and have connected numerous times since graduating. He's a mentor and has helped me believe I can succeed in his industry, which is also a goal of mine. He just recently told me we have very similar personalities and calling a meet together would be a fan favorite. Let's face it: it's all about the fans and the fun, something Dean is brilliant at.

I will now be embarking on the other side of gymnastics—the media side.

A full-time job plus a future connection to my sport, my first love.

It finally happened.

Chapter 26
FINAL CONFESSIONS

CONFESSION—*One on One Gets It Done*

I strongly recommend to all parents—whether divorced, happily married, or your garden-variety dysfunctional family—to find a project to share individually with each of your kids. I'm a big fan of one-on-one time. Baba and I still did our wild traveling. And it is the shared love of travel and being together that makes it so special. Dad and son, one-on-one (I rhymed). Olivia and I keep reflecting about how sharing these confessions with you helped us make sense of the past to help you, the reader, navigate what may come next for you. We also want you to understand that you do have options. Don't feel the pressure to always have to do everything together as a family unit or, in our case, a fractured family unit. Binge-watch a TV program, just the two of you. Work out together. It doesn't have to be fancy. Take a road trip. It just has to be time together to connect and keep knowing each other as you both evolve. Give it a try. You may be surprised.

"You're THE GYMNAST"

Olivia interjection: As we sit at lunch, crafting this final chapter, an acquaintance of my dad's was sitting at the table next to ours. When he got up to leave, my dad waves him over and says, "I don't know if you have ever met my daughter, Olivia?

With excitement he replies, "Oh, you're THE GYMNAST."

When he walked away, my dad and I burst out laughing. Talk about timing. We are literally writing this chapter about being called THE GYMNAST and someone walks up and utters the exact words. Talk about the universe listening in.

I no longer have to respond to, "Can you do a flip?" That's so high school.

Now, nonstop, "Oh, you're THE GYMNAST."

Yes, I was a gymnast. Now I am not. I also have other skills, not just gymnastics. But, to the world, for now, I'm THE GYMNAST.

I know it isn't meant to annoy me. People are being effusive and excited about my past career. I get it. I just wish people would understand, being a D-I athlete isn't all great, great fun. There is a tremendous amount of hardship, emotional and physical pain and doubt, doubt if you can get back up again after a fall and doubt if you can even continue to train and compete.

When you say, "You're the gymnast," do you want me to unload on all that it took to be "THE GYMNAST?"

I also find myself a bit angry at times. I never knew what I was missing. Never had the luxury or time to think, "Where would I like to go on vacation?" as I never thought about much outside of my sport and my schoolwork. Again, great for my need of "structure." Not so great for my ability to draw on "life experience," as you know all my experience.

But it's really okay—Come on over and say, "You're THE GYMNAST!"

JIM INTERJECTION: Really. You find your description annoying? Try this on.

"Oh, you're THAT TRAINER."

Olivia, you got a "the." Why do I get a "that?" For over three decades, I've been in this industry. Yes, I have been a personal trainer, but why do we have to put a "that" in front of it?

My opinion? There is a perception, as Olivia previously wrote; I'm judging. I'm not. I give speeches all the time and say to my audience, if I believe they can handle it:

"Grow up and own your behavior. If you want to eat crap and look like crap (like I did for my first two decades), then don't do crap about it. Just don't complain about it, and I won't give a crap about it either. It's your choice. *No* judgement."

But when I walk into a restaurant, I hear some collective groans. I went to a holiday house party a few years back and entered the front door on the lower level. The party was upstairs on the main floor. Suddenly the staircase was filled with people blocking my way. Why? Many of the guests, the majority of which were my clients, were tossing their overflowing plates of food in the garbage.

Why must we label? Olivia and I are trying to understand, and we may need your help. What is Olivia supposed to say when someone says, "You're THE GYMNAST?" You are going to have to ask her.

With regard to me, I've just accepted it. No, I'm not an author, and notice I'm not even touching the #1 *New York Times* issue. No, I'm not an entrepreneur, who didn't really know what that word meant back when I fell into and started not one, but two businesses. Speaker, nope, just THAT TRAINER.

I do believe everything in life happens for a purpose. Maybe we are challenged by these labels in order to help each other determine what we do next. I don't know. Only time will tell.

THE GYMNAST and THAT TRAINER in Public

Since turning twenty-one, Olivia is now able to go out and have some wine, or a Cosmo, her homage to *Sex and the City*. I frequently like to sit at the bar, which she can now legally do. I also like corner tables or corner booths. Sometimes with my arm around her chair, we laugh as I drink my martini to her Cosmo, and we share shrimp cocktail, fresh crab cakes, sushi, salmon, veggies, a baked potato—whatever. Frequently, the bartender, waiter, or waitress give us a "look," as in, "What's the deal here?" Other patrons literally point and mouth across the table, "What do you think is going on over there?" This happens virtually every time we are out, especially when we are a little dressed up.

Olivia takes charge, and she will finally say, "You know, he's my *dad*," again in the tone I've described. At least this time it's directed at another person.

We were recently invited to a fancy, New York dinner in a private dining room. We walk into the cocktail area, dressed up, and two women in attendance immediately look us up and down and gave us, "the look." Once we finally sat down at the dinner table after the cocktail hour, I went and knelt down in between the two women and said, "I bet you think she's my date." Then paused for their reaction.

Confessions of a DIVISION-I ATHLETE

"It's actually my daughter."

They laughed and said in unison, "date" was their first assumption.

I'm also incredibly proud of how Olivia carries herself. Again, you have to compete around me as I'm "big." I love it when she takes over and captivates other party guests and me with stories, her own observations, her past experience. She never mentions her sport. Oh no, that is my job:

"Did you know Olivia was a star gymnast at Michigan the past four years?"

I know how to give her just a little push, then let her take it from there. Now she's not just my daughter. Her own social capital just took a bump up. She's got her own identity. This is the conversation starter. I then watch her take off.

Since she graduated, I have diligently been working on Olivia's grown-up wardrobe. When we unpacked the six suitcases and four boxes in her New York apartment, I keep pulling out everything "Michigan." Where are the adult clothes I bought her? I see her filling her drawers with a ton of Lululemon. Then rompers. More rompers. Hate rompers. Then more Michigan warmups, sweatshirts, shorts, sports bras, on and on and on.

What is she going to wear to a job interview?

Since they were old enough to understand, my kids have heard me use certain Greek words or phrases, most of them not nice words or phrases. A gentleman is an *anthropo*, and a woman of sophistication, style, and manners is a *kiria*. These are two of my favorites.

We go shopping. I love to shop. Olivia shows me a sweatshirt or comfy sweater. My temperature starts to rise.

"Honey, we are here for adult clothes."

"But dad, it's so soft." This is a nice "dad," not "dad!"

"Put it down, get over here, and go try this on."

I'm happy to say, Olivia now has an appropriate wardrobe befitting of a twenty-four-year-old *kiria*. Let's hope she doesn't only wear it when

I'm around. Oh, and heels. These are going to have to be worn strategically as we told you, she has *no* tendons in her right ankle, and the left calf, ankle and foot are a little wonky since all the injuries occurred on the right. Therefore, she has been putting added pressure on the left. I recently was watching *The View* and saw a segment on Oprah's Favorite Things and bought not one, but four bottles of a lidocaine foot cream for women who experience pain when wearing heels. Olivia told me it works. I "did it!" Let's also hope stem cell research or some new techniques help repair a lot of the damage on her body, feet, ankles, wrists, back, and shoulders.

"Did I miss anything?"

"No, Dad (again said nicely); that's it."

It's time to close. Actually, it's tough to close. As Olivia described after her last gymnastics competition when they didn't advance to the finals, first she felt relief. Then sadness. I'm happy we finished this project since we have no more time.

But I'm also sad. This "structure" in now gone. We would get up, eat, write, go workout, eat lunch while writing (often chicken fajitas, dry, with only lettuce, tomato, salsa, and guacamole on the side, in tortillas), home and go at it a little more. Then we binge-watched *The Marvelous Mrs. Maisel*, *The Crown*, *Jane the Virgin*, or whatever we agreed upon. Jane, who aspires to be a writer, totally inspired us so we need to say a special, "thank you" to the producers of that show. We actually always agreed on what to watch. Come to think of it, there was no hissing or Greek expletives.

Olivia interjection: I have to add for all *Maisel* fans, I bought a cloth tape measure on Amazon Prime to channel my inner Midge. Those of you who are fans will understand.

Our shared purpose, writing, is ending once we successfully respond to the edits. Then it will be put to rest until the publication day and the next purpose, promoting it, will start. But I don't want to gloss over this moment and focus on the future.

Instead, I want to celebrate the win, and "Win the Day." We "did it." We wrote a book together. We "persevered," but this time, together, as part of "the team." Yes, for this fact, the fact we completed something we only flirted with in the past, I am very proud.

I'm going to take a deep breath and enjoy this moment. A big, deep breath, as I have missed so many moments in the past. Not this time.

We are Jim Karas and Olivia Karas, dad and daughter. We survived this important piece in both of our lives.

Thank you for letting us share our *Confessions*.

Chapter 27
FINAL OLIVIA THOUGHTS

CONFESSION—*"I don't have a crystal ball." (Bev Plocki)*

That's what Bev always said at practice. While I was an athlete, I found it annoying. Obviously no one has a crystal ball. But as I've had a lot of time to think about many things (haven't we all?), including the future of gymnastics during this challenging time, I realize her phrase perfectly applies.

Thoughts race through my head:

- How are they going to sanitize a beam after each routine? Sure, beam isn't hard enough already; now let's just make it a Slip 'N Slide.
- How will the athletes, coaches, and support staff stay safe?
- What will it be like for any athlete to finish a great routine or great play and not be able to hug, high five, or slap another player on the back?
- Do we wear masks when we train and compete?

I struggle with the phrase "everything happens for a reason" because some things just seem so random, cruel, and difficult to digest that you can't fathom why they happen. The pandemic is one of them. I was lucky. I got my last season (and we know that was something). I got my senior dinner. My fellow Michigan athletes who missed their final season were devastated. I heard over and over again from all the athletes, "Why is this happening to us?" Now, if I were one of those athletes and someone said to me, "Everything happens for a reason," I'd probably lose it.

I truly believe many situations in life are what you make of them. If you fall off the beam, how do you handle it? If a global pandemic hits and life becomes extremely unpredictable, how do you handle it? I think I have the answer—or at least part of the answer. You get back up. Yep. It sounds cliché, but it's true. You don't let a situation define you. No, you are not "Beam Fall Becky" or "Pandemic Patty." You are you. Own that.

To all my fellow athletes trying to figure out what comes next, I can't possibly understand what you are going through. I know you don't do gymnastics "light," so your discipline to all things gymnastics must be astounding. Plus, doing a floor routine in a mask must surely be brutal. Playing any sport in a mask must be brutal.

My former teammate and good friend Annie Maxim recently told me that when she transferred from Michigan State to Michigan, she would work to prove herself every day. And I think that's what this season and the coming uncertain seasons of gymnastics are going to be. Do it for yourself to prove you're the best athlete, student, teammate, and friend you can be. You aren't doing it for the fans or the judges or the social media gymnastics fans—the "gymternet"—you're doing it for you, the athlete. Be national championship worthy every day even if you don't get to compete for a national championship.

As for me, I'm unfortunately "on a break" with New York City. My dad helped me end my lease early and put everything in storage until it's time to return, whenever that may be. I'm now splitting my time between my mom's house, my dad's house, and some safe travel when I can. I'm cooking more than usual, doing some running to stay mentally and physically in shape, and have become scarily obsessed with *The Crown* and all things royal, including going so far as to adopt an adorable four-year-old corgi named Toni Smith (after my ninety-two-year-old grandmother). I continue to love my work at Huge, learning all things PR and corporate communications, and I am excited to keep writing about my sport for some gymnastics publications. Oh, and the brightest part: amidst watching some of the best musicals from the 1950s with my dad, he surprised me and switched his chairs in the command positions.

So now, I swivel.

ABOUT THE AUTHORS

Jim Karas

After graduating with a BS in Economics from the Wharton School of the University of Pennsylvania, Jim first worked for Merrill Lynch on the Chicago Board Options Exchange. Then in New York, he was the assistant to the president and editor-in-chief of *LEADERS* magazine. If you happened to see *The Devil Wears Prada*, Jim performed the same type of job as Anne Hathaway's character but did so without a cell phone, the internet, or texting. His next stint landed him a job as a private portfolio manager.

In 1987, Jim became one of the first personal trainers in Chicago, created Jim Karas Intelligent Fitness & Wellness, and built a team of trainers and massage therapists. His personal clientele has included Hugh Jackman and Diane Sawyer in addition to numerous business and entertainment leaders. He also created Chicago CryoSpa, which at the time was the first business in Chicago to offer cryotherapy and the eighth in the country. After the publication of his first book in 2001, the #1 *New York Times* bestseller *The Business Plan for the Body*, Jim's speaking, writing, and media career (he was an ABC News contributor) quickly followed. *Confessions* marks Jim's seventh book.

In his spare time, Jim collects art, trades stock, and works out but insists it's much more for his brain than for his body.

For more information, check out jimkaras.com.

ABOUT THE AUTHORS

Olivia Karas

Olivia was a gymnast for over 16 years. Her most rewarding time was when she represented the University of Michigan as a four-time All American and earned four Big Ten championships. She always wanted to be part of a team , and Michigan gave her just that.

Currently, Olivia is an Associate Communications Manager for Huge, a global digital marketing firm. In addition, she has been an on-air commentator for the Big Ten Network, written for gymnastics publications, and participated in Beam Queen Bootcamps with some of her favorite fellow former gymnasts and friends.

Olivia has learned to snow ski and loves it, especially as it was forbidden during her gymnastics career. She spent last summer reading feverishly and has started making her own pickles.

She recently adopted a four-and-a-half-year-old Pembroke Welsh Corgi, who she has lovingly renamed "Toni Smith" after her amazing ninety-two-year-old grandmother. They formed an instant bond, and Toni Smith will soon be returning to New York City with Olivia.